CHANGE YOUR POSTURE

Women!

Empowered Women Empower WOMEN

WITH EDITS BY

AISHA Z. BROCK
REGINA N. ROBERTS
YOLANDA M. MITCHELL

CHANGE YOUR POSTURE *for Women*!
Empowered Women EMPOWER WOMEN

Copyright © 2019 by Sh'Shares NETWORK, LLC.

All rights reserved. No portion of this publication may be reproduced, distributed, or transmitted in any form or by any means, including photocopying, recording, or other electronic or mechanical methods, without the prior written permission of the publisher, except in the case of brief quotations embodied in critical reviews and certain other noncommercial uses permitted by copyright law.

For permission requests, write to the publisher, addressed "ATTN: Permissions" at the following:

Sh'Shares NETWORK, LLC
PO BOX 13202
Jacksonville, FL 32206-0202
http://ShShares.com

Bulk discounts are available on quantity purchases by associations, corporations, and others for business, educational and ministry use. for details, contact the publisher at the address above.

Library of Congress Control Number: 2019917108

ISBN: 978-1-942650-42-3 (Paperback)
ISBN: 978-1-942650-43-0 (eBook)

Printed in the United States of America
FIRST EDITION

To God, the Father:
I am Grateful.
I am Humbled.
I am Yours.
Use Me!

To All God's Beautiful Women:
May this book express all good things that have been shared
with us by mothers, grandmothers, our sisters,
and our new friends.

No woman
ever meets another woman
who is not a friend.

Our unity lives deeper than blood.
D Nicole Williams

contents!

How good and pleasant it is when
sisters
dwell together in unity.

Psalm 133:1

note to readers

Change Your Posture! Change Your LIFE!

This mantra came as a result of my personal endeavor to reposition my*self* and my *mind*. Years before starting this project, I found myself in a frustratingly loooooooong valley of STAGNATION! I was at a numbing standstill—mentally, emotionally, spiritually, physically and otherwise. I had lost my mojo! It was COMPLETELY gone, and it apparently did NOT want to be found!!! Eeeek!

Increasingly, I became tired! I was tired of *being* tired, and all of that made me even *more* tired! As much as I *thought* I was doing, from the looks of it all, it seemed that I was doing absolutely NOTHING! Seemingly, I was making NO progress at all! My encouragement was that I KNEW I had somewhere I wanted to be in life, and I knew that I couldn't embark on a "casual" journey to get there. My lofty dreams required effort, inspiration and ACTION that matched the weight of my purpose. in effect, I had to change my own posture to change my own life!

That is EXACTLY what I am urging each of you to do with this series of books: **Change Your Posture! Change Your LIFE!** Be a firm believer in passionate pursuit of purpose! Take the time needed to CREATE the life of your dreams using ALL that you've been given! Commit yourself to your future RIGHT NOW letting no excuse stand in the way of attainment. by everything that has been instilled within you, you owe it to yourself to be GREAT! JUST DO IT! Don't wait another day.

To start from the beginning, let's review the question: *What is an affirmation?*

★ Affirmations are positive statements made audibly so that the soul can hear. Consider affirmations a practice of mind-bending. with the goal of directing your mind to new thought and your body to new action, you affirm aloud for practical communication with your spirit man.

★ The spirit of a man controls his destiny, so affirmers don't make these statements casually. Each declaration calls for passionate conviction and mental commitment to the chosen affirmation. No empty statements here!!! State your affirmations in FULL belief of their TRUTH!

★ Following audible recitation of the affirmations, participate in the journal entries and occasional "Woman's Work" to fully vest yourself in the chosen declaration.

★ You'll get the MOST out of this book by following closely along in your journal since you will increase your self-awareness along the way.

Now, this book makes it reeeeeeeeallly really easy for you to follow along and clearly affirm, decree AND declare each day's statements.

Self-help is truly what it says it is: *Self. Help.* Self-help calls into question the things that you are willing to do for yourself. Even with a formal life coach, inspirational audio-visuals and all the leadership books in the world, it is ALL for naught if you won't help yourself! Commit yourself to each moment, and no matter what happens, don't you EVER quit!

Don't STOP! GET IT! GET IT!

Change Your Posture! Change Your LIFE!

thanks!

acknowledgements

___FIRST AND FOREMOST…

To the many women who have contributed to this book: Arielle Griffin (my mentee), my dear mother Elder Loretta "LoLo" Stoney (I love you!), my lovely sister Monique Denise, Cortney Surrency (my cousin), Dr. Latisha D. Reeves Henry (my most honorable mentor 😊), Rev. Victoria Hamilton (my spiritual leader, my heart, my friend, and the list goes on…), Brittany Whigham (my friend), Carolyn Thompson (my other mother), Chantell Williams (my 3rd sister), Clemmie Thompson (THE truth!), Erika Harp (my friend), my auntie Freda Wells, Minister Gail Engram, Kelly Gardner (you keep the *entire* section together with your example!), Kenajawa Woody (a Godsend!), Kwanza Yates (my loving and lovable friend), Coach Latoya Kight (my 2nd sister), LeLeatha Mitchell (my SPICY cousin), my protégé Coach Mechelle Canady, my dear friend Coach Monique Carter, Lady Stephanie Hamilton Muwunganirwa (my newest sister), and Coach Regina Roberts without whom none of this would have *ever* been possible…

Words cannot express to you the depth of my thanks and sincere gratitude for all you have contributed to this process. Lord knows I am utterly grateful for your roles and your deep patience with me through this journey together. I don't take lightly the amount of trust you gave as I pushed and pulled and tugged (*and sometimes begged!*), but… HERE WE ARE! I can't believe it's finally HERE!!!!!!! I am SO excited and blessed to have the fortune of sharing this path with you. Deep thanks and MUCH love!

—*Coach D!*

___TO MY SISTER...

Monique, I love you like no other... NO other. You are an inspiration to me every day, in every way. I remember, as a little sister, looking up to you. I just loved your spirit and your untamed JOY! You TRULY were a light back then. Now... you have been the foremost reason for my joy of the learning truths about ALL women!

Your life has taught me SO many lessons—not all of which were a pleasure to you—but, trust... I have learned more than we could ever quantify. YOU, my sister, are one *very* qualified teacher. Thanks for all that you are. Thanks for the way you have walked. Thanks for being willing to take some tumbles (and sometimes rolling down WHOLE, entire mountains) so that I, and LoLo, could learn from you. Through you, we learned resistance. Through you, learned resilience. Through you, we learned resolve.

Thanks for being my hope. Thanks for being my light. Thanks for being my sister.

forward!

by Rev. Victoria L Hamilton

I had been out of church for 12 years...

It was 1997.

That's when God called me.

I was called to walk with my husband in ministry. He had heard the call too. We answered.

Before pastoring, we returned to the church and served for 10 years. Before *that*… I had been out of church for 12 years, and God still saw fit to use me. on April 20, 2002, my husband and I were ordained. Together, we pastored for 22 years.

Now, I am a recently retired rostered pastor in the Evangelical Lutheran Church in America (ELCA). Being rostered means I am still on "the list" of ordained pastors along with others. At age 68, I have reached retirement age and—at this time—needed to come out of parish ministry. *(My zeal had left me.)* I do plan on, however, working and volunteering within social action ministries that need voices to speak for those who may not be able to speak for themselves. Often, I am called to speak for those who don't have the finances or those who need to be listened to. There are also those who need love despite all imperfections they believe they have; these are those who need to see themselves as unique givers…

When my spouse William, aka "P. Ham," asked my mom about marriage, the first thing she said was, "Why?"

P. Ham said, "I love your daughter."

Mother said, "Oh. This is serious."

She looked at me. She said, "And don't say I was your age when I got married. You see where I am now."

At age 32, my mother was a divorcée with five children—girls—and I was the oldest at 15. Her stipulations where that I: 1, finish high school; 2, get some kind of higher education; and 3, get a job so that when the babies started coming, I would not have to grieve what I had never done! *(Oh, and my husband had to reach the rank of E4 to be able to afford me.)* 😊

November of 2019 marks our 50th year of marriage. When we married, I was 18 and my husband was 20. I got married in Detroit. I then moved to California where my husband was stationed in the U.S. Navy. We had been engaged for 2 years.

Through a few moves, I met many women of all cultures and from many different states and countries. Despite this, I still found myself lonesome many times—especially in ministry. I knew plenty women and I quickly found that *all* women need encouragement—not just me, a young woman of 20 living in what felt like a foreign country.

Back then, making a telephone call was nowhere near as easy as it is today. I had few connections; that's because we were all so fresh in the world. Any affirmation we *did* receive were not because of experience, per se, but because we simply needed to learn how to survive. A resource such as CHANGE YOUR POSTURE FOR *Women! Empowered Women* EMPOWER WOMEN was never available. to have had a book with words of encouragement, on so many topics, with so many voices… would have been such a benefit for me back then. It is a publication for tomorrow's ladies, our granddaughters, nieces, aunts, moms, and our daughters as well. the voices you will meet are those of our friends and our elders. They are full of wisdom and shared personal experiences.

In today's world, women are still learning to reach out to one another the best way they can. It doesn't matter how young you are, or your life's experiences to date, **we as women can still learn from one another to help make one another whole.** My prayer for you as you read this book is that you continue to look inside yourself asking, "WHO might I have a positive impact on? WHAT changes do I need to make? WHEN can I begin my transformation? WHERE do I want to see changes and WHERE can my voice be heard?" Overall, you should ask, "WHY has God called me to make a difference?"

I am really blessed to have been asked to be a part of this project. the project challenged me as an elder of the group. My esteem has been lifted *as all I thought I was good for was a decent sermon!* You will be encouraged as you read the words by women for women to empower us all. Peace, love, joy and prayers to each of you.

I am a daughter, sister, wife, and a mother to William, Stephanie, and my Godson Charles. Their spouses are Autumn, Panashe and Amber. My little hearts—who are growing up on me—are Sekai, Nyasha, Francisca, Miles, and Noah.

Thank you, Coach D Nicole Williams, for this opportunity.

—Rev. Victoria L. Hamilton
Listed herein as MommyV

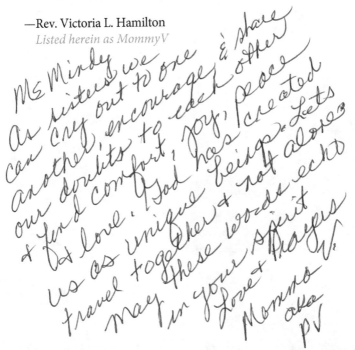

Ms Mindy
As sisters we can cry out to one another, encourage & share our doubts to each other & find comfort, joy, peace & love. God has created us as unique being & not alone. Lets travel together & may these words echo in your spirit in Love & Prayers
MommyV aka PV

Soul!

January

I Am A Woman of Prayer

"And Hannah answered and said,
No my lord, I am a woman of a sorrowful spirit:
I have drunk neither wine nor strong drink,
but have poured out my soul before the Lord."
I Samuel 1:15 KJV

Hannah prayed because of deeply entrenched hunger, an insatiable thirsting that could find no ordinary relief. She desperately needed to birth a child in a patriarchal society that valued women primarily on their ability to help reproduce. What an excruciating moment to realize that your purpose is eluding you, and you feel powerless to grab hold of it. That's how she felt with barrenness tightening its grip like a noose smothering and draining life from her soul. Every season, she traveled to worship at the temple without the coveted evidence of what her culture deemed a fruitful and blessed marriage. It became harder to breathe, to live, and to thrive without a child, so Hannah did the only thing she could have done: she fervently prayed.

"And there was one Anna, a prophetess,
the daughter of Phanuel, of the tribe of Asher;
she was of great age, and had lived with a
husband seven years from her virginity; And
she was a widow of about fourscore and four
years, which departed not from the temple,
but served God with fastings and prayers
night and day."
Luke 2:36-38 KJV

Next, we find Anna, who was always in the temple praying and fasting because, even at an old age, she resolved to live her faith. As a woman of God—a prophetess—she was a woman of prayer. This was her life because she had resolved that she would praise the Lord and spread the word that the Redeemer has come to Jerusalem. After praying and fasting, offering the totality of herself in relationship with her Father, she received the ultimate answer. the Redeemer showed up.

Whether we are desperately grieving, or anticipating with joy the movement of God, the answer is always prayer. It centers and grounds us, giving us a place to rest in calm and a pillar to fortify us in the storm. I thrive in the posture of prayer; it is a praying spirit that makes me ever cognizant of God's presence with us, and certainly, sister-girlfriends, we all need that.

— Dr. Latisha D. Reeves Henry

January

I Am a Child of God!

You can't make RIGHT decisions from the wrong place. We must keep a sound mind so we can make the best decisions for our lives. We must stay in the will of God to experience unyielding success or prosperity. Your enemies become your footstool because even their best thinking from that wrong place can only lead to destructive decisions for them. They will put their best plans together to destroy you, but how successful can those plans be when they come from a place of evil, hate, shame, immaturity, and selfishness? In this case, the weapon formed against you can't prosper because they are created from shabby tools and supplies manufactured in anger and hate.

Any person who ever works against you is not thinking clearly. They have missed a critical element: You are a child of God! So be encouraged, stay in prayer, seek the truth, expect victory, spread love, and glorify God!

— Kwanza Yates

Say Aloud: **I Am a Child of God!**

January 3

No Situation Is Too Much
Once I Realize Who Holds the Power

I was once told that if you are continually presented with the same circumstance, God wants you to see that you didn't do something right the first time. This reminds me of when we were younger, and our parents made us do a task until we get it done right. This stands true for circumstances that we continually put ourselves in. Once we receive Christ as our Lord and Savior, we are also free from bondage.

★ Am I in a toxic relationship that God has said I don't need to be in, but I just can't figure out why the relationship is so hard?

★ Do I feel that I can never catch a break financially?

I Peter 5:7 tells us, "Give all your worries and cares to God, for He cares about you." This scripture lets me know that no matter what I go through in life, God has the power to take care of it.

You will know that *no* situation is too much once you realize who holds all the power!

— Kenajawa LaShawn

Affirmation Journal
★ What can I change about my painful situations in life?
★ How can I involve God into my process?
★ How will I involve God into my process?

Say Aloud: **No Situation Is Too Much**

January 4

" I Believe the Impossible Is Possible! "

Have you ever been told that life isn't a fairytale? But why can't it be!?

When you are aligned or dialed into God and His will for your life, you begin to trust that your desires are His original wants and expectations for your life. We get into situations of disappointment when we make decisions outside of His precious will. Being tuned in to God provides a sense of confidence that you are doing the right thing, and even when it looks impossible, you have to believe what you know and trust that God's promise will become reality because you have confidence.

Ultimately, you must confirm your trust in God and build your faith in yourself. You are He and He is you. I intentionally stated it that way because we must start believing that He has given us the same abilities that He possesses. This is an odd concept to grasp because the world will tell you that there are limits to life where Gods tells you that what you want and what you receive in life is limitless, so get dialed in!

Get dialed in so that you can hear and trust what God has promised you. Start living the fairytale God has for your life! Believe the impossible is possible!

— Cortney D. Surrency, AC-CHC

Say Aloud: I Believe the Impossible Is Possible!

January 5

"The Source of My Supply Is Limitless"

Ask yourself, "What is too hard for my God?" Your first response might be to actually think about this, and you will probably think along the terms of your own limits. You will probably think about your current bank account. You will probably reflect upon all your worldly possessions, and then you might realize how very little you have. Hopefully, you will arrive at a point in your thought process where you remember that the question was about God; it was never about you!

Now your mind begins to expand exponentially. You think about the country you live in. Then, you expand out into the world, and finally, to the universe. SO, what is it? What is too hard for MY God? Hmmm...?

If He could simply speak the universe into existence, then truly, what is too hard for God?

The answer: Nothing, for the God I serve is limitless.

— Kwanza Yates

January 6

"I Will Have Faith Without Borders"

Faith without borders requires us to be brave, to trust God, and to live life boldly, proclaiming our faith in God no matter what. God commands us to have faith without borders. God tells us that if you ask in Jesus' name, "I will give it to you." That is so powerful. If you ask in Jesus' name, and you are in the will of God, you will have it. That means NOTHING—I mean nothing—is impossible!

If God asks you to heal, and you're obedient, you can heal the sick. You can raise the dead. That may sound strange, but God gives us the same authority as His son who did miraculous things.

Get in tuned to your spiritual gifts so that God can show you that you have the ability to do the impossible. Start believing that you can do the impossible because you can if you truly believe, and your desire is in the will of God.

— Cortney D. Surrency, AC-CHC

7

January

"

I Can Do All Things Through Christ

"

I Can Do All Things Through Christ!

Most of us hear this affirmation and think that God will miraculously make our hopes and dreams a reality. We think that by doing all things through Christ, our business will immediately flourish, we will effortlessly pass the test, and a miracle in our finances will just fall down from heaven above. If we think about the context of what Paul was talking about in this time, this scripture had nothing to do with prosperity. This in no way insinuates that

God cannot bless you, but this scripture should be used to get us through some of the toughest times in our journey.

At age 20, when I delivered a stillborn child and had only been a Christian for six months, I needed God's strength to help me to continue to hold on and to understand what was happening in my life. So, when this scripture says I can do all things through Christ who strengthens me, it means that the same strength will help me through the days when depression is getting the best of me, and I know I can't do it alone. God's strength will carry me through times when I don't understand what is happening in life.

— Kenajawa LaShawn

January

I Will Live in the Surplus

God wants us to have more. I don't know what Bible some people are reading because the God in the Bible I read wants us to live in the overflow. That doesn't always mean money. God can want us to have financial freedom or may proclaim that our house will be paid off in a year, but the ultimate desire is for us to live abundantly. God wants to meet every heart's desire because he wants the BEST for us! This means that shying away from your dreams by saying, "They are too big," or "That will never happen," is really showing your disobedience to what God has planned for your life. Not living in the surplus is being disobedient. Living in fear or choosing to feel like you don't deserve more is not God's language.

So, think about it...

What do you have to lose?

Nothing! Because when you're with Him, you can never lose. He just requires us to ask, receive, and believe, and LOVE, in the surplus!

— Cortney D. Surrency, AC-CHC

January

" I Make Time for and Embrace My Blessings! "

Instead of focusing on what's wrong in your life, start to look around you and count all the things you have to be grateful for! Consider what's *right* with you. Are you breathing? Have food to eat? A roof over your head? Family and friends who love you? Well, you're doing a lot better than most! Remember when that was all that mattered? *I know we're a long way from simplicity now, but don't forget simplicity!*

Next, it's crucial we take the time to talk to and truly LISTEN to our loved ones. Ask about their day, goals, interests, and what makes them happy. Ask them, "How can I be a better *me*, for you?" Pay attention to signs of change *(good or bad)* in your home. *Did you know there was a rise of depression in children?* Show your children their worth.

Finally, regarding your space—whether it's a room, apartment, or a house—give it some TLC and appreciation. You know the saying, "You'll never get what you want until you appreciate and take care of what you already have." Your job, career, your business... appreciate it all! Not the job you want? Make a change, but make sure you're not burning bridges while you're there; rather, create a broad network instead.

— Monique Carter

January

" I Will Ask! I Will Receive! I Will Believe! "

When we ask God for something, we often think we have to sit around and wait for it to be given to us. That's because we don't know that really—in the spirit—we already have it! the moment we ask, we receive it. How wonderful that the asking and receiving is simultaneous! God has already given us the desires of our heart, but He requires us to ask. Then our faith helps is puts our belief in what God has told us into action.

Once you ask in the spirit, it is yours! Now, you have to trust what you heard, and no matter what comes your way, believe what has been told to you. We like to think of God as a genie. Instead, we should understand that God is outside of time and space. Something may feel like years to us when it's only moments for God.

Trust your Father and know that He already knows the perfect moment in time where your blessing will become reality.

— Cortney D. Surreney, AC-CHC

Say Aloud: **I Will Ask! I Will Receive! I Will Believe!**

January 11

I Make Room for My Blessings

What's holding you back? Could it be the very things you are holding on to? This is a physical, mental, and *spiritual* discussion.

First, consider the physical. Look around you. Is your home surrounded by clutter and disorganization? Is your room overflowing with chaos? What about your workspace? Are their papers everywhere? Books, folders, and sticky notes in excess?

Everything has its place. Now, perfect organization is not required, but when we continue to put things out of place and attempt to function in disorder, this could serve as a representation that there are things in our unseen life that are also out of place. We often don't see how disorganization and clutter in our physical lives affect us and cause a vicious cycle of disarray and blessing blockage in our spiritual lives.

Today, take some time and unclutter your surroundings. Make room for the blessings to flow in every area of your life.

— Kwanza Yates

This Woman's Work [Today]

* Stop what you're doing now and schedule out some time *today* to declutter.
* Don't worry about getting BIG work done.
* Don't make it a huge project.
* Move things to their proper places.
* Evaluate how you feel when you're done.
* Make sure to note how you felt *before* the tidying.

Affirmation Journal

* What areas of my life need decluttering?
* How can decluttering on a regular basis help me make room for blessings in my life?

January

My Connection with God Is SECURE!

I have a few spiritual sisters that I trust with my whole heart. When they tell me something, I believe them. What freedom to have because of them! I know they are aligned with the Holy Spirit, so when they share, I know that it's not their words but the word of God through the Holy Spirit.

At times when you hear directions, you may often think, "Is that me, Lord, or is it you?" You can move with confidence when you know that you are aligned with God because your words are His words, your thoughts are His thoughts. When I need to make a decision, I am confident in what has been said to me because of the connection I have with Him. So, if you know your connection is not secure with God, begin today and ask God to increase your bond. You will find that the Holy Spirit will start to speak loudly to you where you can no longer deny the answer. You will also find that God sends you confirmation along the way.

The moment you realize that your connection is secure, you can begin to trust yourself with confidence and watch God move in your life!

— Cortney D. Surrency, AC-CHC

Say Aloud: **My Connection with God Is SECURE!**

January 13

"I Know Him for Myself"

If you do nothing else, get to know God...

FOR YOURSELF!

When I was growing up, I remember the elders of the church saying, "You don't know God like I know God!" That used to confuse me. Aren't we all serving the same God?

Think about your relationship with a close girlfriend. You know her, but you don't know her as her mother knows her, like her child's father knows her, or even like her daughter knows her. These are all different relationship connections experienced in a unique way between them. on your journey, you were meant to experience her as a close friend—not as a mother or daughter.

The same occurs with God: who He is and what He has done for and revealed to me may not be the same for you. Our conversations are different, and my heart's desires are different. He meets me where I am, and He will meet you where you are. He created us as individuals that are spiritually connected and bonded in eternity. How awesome is that?

We are like individual charms on a bracelet; each charm has its own unique story that's connected to this journey on the spiritual chain of life, but you can't get connected until you get to know Him for yourself.

— Kwanza Yates

Say Aloud: **I Know Him for Myself**

I Will Seek God's Counsel

We usually go to God after we are desperate and already in a mess. Think about it...

If you would have stopped and asked God about the guy you in were interested in dating from the start, He may have given you an answer that could have saved you a lot of heartache and pain. Next time try seeking God's counsel before jumping into action.

Start by seeking God's assistance with everyday decision making. From purchasing new pots and pans to purchasing a home, seek God's opinion in everything thing that you do. Your everyday decisions impact not only your journey through life, but everyone who is in association with you. by listening to your spirit about not rushing out the house, you could be avoiding a car accident.

Seeking God's counsel doesn't have to be this long, drawn-out prayer, and it doesn't take fasting or meditation. Even though these things are great resources of clarity, most times, seeking God means simply asking what you will, in Jesus' name, and trusting yourself.

You can have confidence in your intuition when you are fully locked into God, and when He abides in you, He will take care of your needs.

— Cortney D. Surrency, AC-CHC

Say Aloud: **I Will Seek God's Counsel**

January 15

God is the Author of My Life.
I Am the Publisher.

God writes the stories of our days and our nights. He created us in His image and allows us to walk the earth in His greatness. He sees into our future, and He puts our past transgressions into the seas of forgetfulness. He dwells in us so that His will may be done, on earth, as it is in heaven. He pours into us the light of love, the words of wisdom, and the knowledge of the truth, and then, He gives us the publishing rights. He gives us the freedom to go forth into the land and spread the good word. And He also gives us the freedom to go forth into the land and stand against evil. He gives us the publishing rights--the ability to walk out His greatness in our own way or to live as fully as His original manuscript intended.

New days, new mercies, new chapters He gives us, all the days of our lives. And all the days of our lives, we get to decide what gets published into the world.

— Kwanza Yates

Affirmation Journal

★ What does it mean to say God is author of my life?
★ What does it mean to say I am publisher?
★ How can I ensure my life is a quality publication?
★ How can I continually be an original manuscript of his perfect creation?

Say Aloud: **God is the Author of My Life. I Publish It.**

I Am the Vessel, Not the Source of My Power. To the Higher One, I Surrender.

We have probably all heard the scripture, "I can do all things through Him who gives me strength." *(That's Philippians 4:13.)* But the question is: Do you believe it?

When we understand the source of our power, we understand how much power we have. Things for me are so much easier since I depend on the power of God. It wasn't until I surrendered to God that my power was unleashed. I remember, towards the end of 2018, I was overcoming a low moment in life. I had lost my job, and I wasn't able to continue school because I couldn't pay anymore. I was also going through a writer's block with my writing, so I decided to take a deep look into my relationship with Christ. I had to evaluate why I felt so detached in life, even though I was still connected with God.

After taking some much-needed time with God, I realized I was leaning on my own power and not the power of God. That's why I was feeling a lack in my relationship with Christ and was experiencing so much anxiety from life. After this experience, I always remind myself: anytime I depend on myself, I will not make it.

I need my Father's power to make it.

— Kenajawa LaShawn

Affirmation Journal

★ **What does this mean?**
   "I can do all things through Him who gives me strength."
★ **What does it mean to say God will give me strength?**
★ **Do I believe I can do all things through Christ?**
★ **What adjustments do I need to make?**

January

I Will Have FAITH. . . in My Faith!

For those of us who have grown up in religious settings, we know a thing or two about faith. We are taught about having faith almost from the moment we were born. However, as we age and mature in our faith, we begin to struggle with what having faith actually means. What's worst is that we say we have faith, but when things get really hard, or when things look impossible, we tend to lose faith pret-ty easily. Therefore, having faith in your faith will help you push through the really bad times.

How do you have faith in your faith? You have to stay motivated. the way that you do that is to fill yourself with the word of God. Ask God to lead you to scriptures that will feed your stamina. Secondly, surround yourself around faith-filled people. They will give you a boost when you feel low. They will believe when you don't. And lastly, trust the Most High God. He is unwavering and never changing.

So, the next time you feel your faith wavering, take the time to write down all the many breakthroughs God has provided for you. Keep your thoughts and heart focused on these things, and you will find yourself having a deeper faith in your faithfulness.

— Cortney D. Surrency, AC-CHC

Say Aloud: I Will Have FAITH. . . in My Faith!

I Am Proud of My Faith Practices

Your relationship with God, your higher power, is just like any other relationship—it needs maintaining. Think about it... what would the condition of a relationship be if there was no time spent, no calls or visits unless YOU needed something? Imagine a relationship with no trust, no faith, or no good ole' fashioned TLC?

Relationships NEED restoration! So, how does one restore and maintain their relationship with God *(or your preferred higher power)*? by practicing faith and having good faith habits. the key here is variety. Let's not allow this relationship to become boring and complacent. Consider using a daily devotional or guidebook to help you. This may typically include a single scripture. You can research the scripture by listening to audio or videos on the scripture until you have a clear understanding of its direct impact on YOUR life. Through journaling, you'll be taking note of what you read and reflect on how you feel. Then, finally, say a quick prayer.

Try this daily, preferably, first thing in the morning before anything or anyone has the chance to impact your spirit. This will make the occurrences of the day a bit more manageable.

— Monique Carter

This Woman's Work (Today)

* ★ While you work through this daily devotional, find one for your mate or a close friend to participate in.
* ★ Hold one another accountable to the daily reading.
* ★ Incorporate more faith practices into your daily life.

January 19

" Don't Be Too Ashamed or Too Proud To Pray! "

Since that incident in the garden of Eden, humans have repeatedly proven that we do not like to be uncovered before others. the vulnerability of exposure is paralyzing, and its occurrence brings us shame. Shame produces humiliation that discredits, degrades, and embarrasses us. It makes us feel unworthy and insignificant because of our mistakes and our failures. We are even shameful of the sins committed against us just as well as we are ashamed of those sins we committed on our own, so... we cloak ourselves in secrecy and fig leaf band-aids to put distance between us and the Holy One who is so different from us. in other cases, we decide to pick ourselves up and build a defense, a dense house of cards named pride. This mechanism which masquerades as a walled fortress is only as formidable as a glasshouse tumbling in a rockslide. Pride comes before a great fall and disconnects us from Help and Healing; it blinds us to the destruction that lies in wait.

Though on opposite ends of the spectrum, both shame and pride are detrimental to us; they silence us. They rob us of intimacy while breeding isolation. the antidote to these is time spent in the Word, practicing reflection and submission through prayer.

Never be too ashamed or too prideful to ask for help. Disrobe yourself in prayer before the One who clothes us with dignity and honor through loving restoration. There is no place too low or too high that prayer cannot reach, and love has not covered. Don't be too ashamed or too proud to pray!

— Dr. Latisha D. Reeves Henry

Say Aloud: **I Won't Be Too Ashamed to Pray!**

January

"

I Pray!!!

"

When all is well, I pray. When nothing appears to be going well, I pray. I pray *for*, and in, all things because prayer connects me to God and centers me so that I stay sane.

I pray when clarity escapes me or scares me. I pray when confusion comes until it goes. Prayer is a constant companion of ongoing conversation, dialogue, guidance, and direction for the journey, so... I PRAY!!!

I pray until something happens—either when the evidence of "Yes!" appears and brings me joyous laughter or when I am overwhelmed by the "No!" I never hoped for. I pray because it is the avenue to intimate knowledge and voice recognition of the Voice, the Savior. the *sheep know the voice of the Good Shepherd.*

I pray because it releases and cleanses me of the weight of the cares of the world—not so that we don't care in the end, but because we care deeply, even in the beginning. Prayer provides a blanket that warms the soul.

I pray because prayer works. It changes the situation or our perspective on it. Prayers avail much when spoken—whether in the heart or audibly—from a sincere, surrendered place within. Prayer permeates the toughest, most impenetrable exteriors and interiors. Prayer is healing brought about through conversation. It draws us closer and lifts us higher. I pray because I know that God answers and likes to hear my voice. I pray because life, problems, deferred desires, and dreams demand that I must, but I pray mostly because...

...even though things may stay the way that they are, I most certainly will not.

— Dr. Latisha D. Reeves Henry

Say Aloud: **I Pray!!!**

January

21

I Will BE STILL. . . And Wait on God

Being still is what God requires us to do.

What does that really mean? Should we physically stop taking action or does this mean to spiritually and mentally do nothing?

To be still is to use constraint or silence the mind and heart. Many times, we hear from God, but then we want to control how He fast He moves to give us the blessing that He promised for us. Naturally, out of excitement, you are going around and around in your mind with the possibilities of how the blessing will become your reality when actually you should do nothing. Rest in the glory! Rest knowing that you already have what you desire and believe it knowing that your desires will come to you at the most perfect time. the hard part is done. Believing in the spirit is the hardest part. Now, you must continue to serve while you wait. Focus your energy on serving others and on being a vessel for God. You will see that the more you serve, the more God will send you little blessings to feed your spirit which will in turn help you to continue to be still and wait on God.

— Cortney D. Surreney, AC-CHC

Say Aloud: I Will BE STILL. . . And Wait on God

January

God Sees Me

God calls us according to how He sees us and not according to how we see ourselves. ***THANK the LORD!*** Soooo many outside influences impact the way we see ourselves. Many things on social media factor into our self-image, and when we make comparisons to others, we deny ourselves the ability to view our lives the way God views us.

God sees us, and He knows all about us. God gifted us to impact the world, and we have the ability to change the lives of others by simply being who God created us to be.

If you can't yet see yourself the way God sees you, pray today and say, "God, help me to see me as you see me!" When you begin to see yourself the way God sees you, you will know that there's nothing you cannot do. You will know that you can be more than a conqueror. You will know that you can be the one who changes the lives of those you come in contact with. by seeing yourself as God sees you, you will know that you can be successful. You will know that's how God sees you because that's what His word says. God says you will be the head and not the tail—above and not beneath. You will lack no good thing, and everything that you touch will prosper. God's word also says that *all* things work together for your good—even those things you're ashamed of and afraid to share with others.

Those things that you're ashamed of in no way changed the way God sees you because He sees fit to use your failures. So continually pray to see yourself the way God sees you because He sees you as GREAT!

— Coach Mechelle Canady

Say Aloud: **God Sees Me**

January

When God Lives in My Heart, I Am Never Alone

We live in a time when there are over seven billion people alive—over seven billion people breathing and sharing and experiencing. We also live in a time when people feel alone more than ever before. We are spiritual beings having a human experience. with the advancement of technology, and the continuous increase in population, it is no wonder we seek to have more and more human experiences, yet we are constantly distracted from spiritual experiences.

We must continue to remind ourselves of where it all begins-- continue to remind ourselves of the place where we are truly all connected. It's not on social media, but it is within. We are all connected to the source. We are all connected to the Alpha, and we will all be reunited in the Omega. Until then, we should nurture the relationship with God in our hearts so that we never feel alone.

— Kwanza Yates

January

God Is Great! God Is Good!

God is great!
Good is GOOD!

That is so true. He is AMAAAAAAAAAAAAAAZING!

God cannot fail. God cannot disappoint. I believe in Him so much, and I trust that He has my BEST interest at heart. He does ALL things great because He is great, and no matter how bad I feel, no matter how many times I fall, no matter how disappointed I am, I know that God will always come through.

God is incredible, and I know that as long as He's in my life, everything will be okay. I thank Him for everything He has done, everything He has kept me from, everything He stopped from attacking me. I bless His name for being who He is in my life because He could have chosen someone else. Knowing that He could have overlooked me, but He still chose to pick me makes me absolutely love how He loves me!!!

— Coach Latoya Kight

January

I Want to Feel God's Love

There is a longing, a thirsting in each of us that is insatiable, only to be quenched by God. Many of us have never learned nor were taught how to quiet ourselves in stillness and listen for God's voice and sense God's presence with us and within us.

Luckily, God has shared with us how we can connect. Proverbs 8:17 says, "I love them that love me; and those that seek me early shall find me." This scripture is a picture of the prelude to intimacy. God's love for creation is evident in nature, in our intellect and advancements, in the sun, moon, stars, and planets, in newborn babies and the delight of children. the deeper, more intimate way to feel God's love is to surrender to

His working, His speaking, and His leading as we seek connection.

Relationship is built on surrendered moments of vulnerability. Trust God enough to look at what God says about love, acceptance, and seeking. Trust God enough to ask hard questions and spend time seeking Him in scripture by meditating on its truth *(see John 3:16-17; John 15; Psalm 23; Psalm 139; Psalm 18:2; Isaiah 43:18-19; Psalm 72:26; Zephaniah 3:17; Jeremiah 31:3)*.

Feeling God's love means entering into painful moments of truth about where there is a deficit in our lives and still, we are met with grace. Sit with a journal and a pen, without cell phone or interruption, and ask God to speak simply and clearly. Then write what you think, hear or feel as you spend that time seeking Him. This process takes us through a myriad of emotions where we come to discover that we feel comfort, strength, and love as we hear, heal, and respond in reliant obedience.

We want to feel God's love deeply, so we must respond to God's love as we learn more of it through His word. We learn more as we pray while we experience that love personally in the calming of our spirits, the blessing of healthy relationships, and in the peace of being loved, known, and cared for.

— Dr. Latisha D. Reeves Henry

This Woman's Work (This Week)

- ★ *Read John 15*
- ★ *Read Psalm 23*
- ★ *Read Psalm 139*
- ★ *Journal your thoughts at the end of each reading.*

Say Aloud: I Want to Feel God's Love

"There Is NO Love Like the Love of God!!! "

There is no love like the love of God.
There is NO love like the love of God!!!
It hits you different when you put this TRUTH into action...
when you have to look at yourself in the mirror
and acknowledge who you are
and remember He loves you just as He made you.
He empowers you to love as He does.
He gave you purpose,
and He moves you anyway, even when you hurt!
When you're hurt, you can't really inspire anyone,
but when you feel worthless,
that's exactly when he lifts you UP!!!
He carries you in your stagnant moments,
and He will never let you fall.
Wanna know why?
Because there is **NO** love...
...like the love of **GOD**!

— Stephanie Hamilton Muwunganirwa

Say Aloud: **There Is NO Love Like the Love of God!**

January 27

"

My Affirmations Are Powerful

"

I Have the Power to Speak Things Over My Life!

I can't lie—I didn't always believe in affirmations. I would see people post them, and I was like, "Okay... I can say the words, but it's not going to change anything." This was before I realized the power that my own words held. I now know that the things I speak over my own life hold more power than anything anyone else can speak over my life.

Affirmations are all about mindset! Start today by speaking positivity over your life and continue to speak it until you believe it. **Your affirmations are powerful!** They have the power to change the course of your life... if you believe it.

Here are some of my favorite affirmations:

- ★ I AM SOMEBODY!
- ★ The Power is Within Me!
- ★ I AM IMPORTANT!
- ★ I Can Do All Things Through Him Who Gives Me Strength.
- ★ **I WILL NOT GIVE UP!**

Affirmations are important to me because, in dealing with depression and anxiety, my thoughts can be very dark sometimes. They can sound so real that I confuse them with reality. A simple phrase such as, "DON'T GIVE UP!" reminds me that my suicidal thoughts are not reality. Starting my days with a positive affirmation sets the tone for the rest of my day.

— Kenajawa LaShawn

This Woman's Work (Today)

- ★ Today, write down five affirmational phrases you can reference quickly when you need them.

" I Will NOT Quit "

Quitting is for suckers! I would rather try and lose than never try and still lose. Quitting will leave you wondering what could've been. Quitting means giving up. You could forfeit all your dreams by not continuing what you started. If there is something in you that sparks a fire, don't let that go out—protect it at all costs. Don't block your destiny or the freedom of others by quitting.

No matter the obstacles in your life, fight through them. the enemy will always throw a curveball to try to make you give up. He wants you to lose. He wants you to be down and out. He wants you to live in doubt. He desires for you to have a miserable life. His ultimate goal is to snatch all of your dreams and goals away. There is no way he will ever be okay with you conquering your goals and achieving your purpose, BUT…

Remember: with God on your side, you can achieve whatever you want, so long as you do not quit!

— Coach Latoya Kight

" I Have One Purpose "

Matthew 28:19 defines my purpose:

"Therefore, go and make disciples of all nations, baptizing them in the name of the Father and the Son and the Holy Spirit."

For a long time, I questioned what my purpose was in life. I found myself considering things that I was gifted at, but they did not sustain my interest long. I would lose motivation and constantly battle the mental burden of not being "good enough." Everything changed when, one day, someone helped me to realize that my one purpose is to help others find God like someone helped me find God. All other things I am talented in are tools I can use to help me facilitate this one mission.

So... the next time you start to question your purpose... don't.

As believers, we all have one true purpose *(mentioned above)*. We should use our gifts to help facilitate that mission. Since I have learned this, it is easier to operate in my writing and in my business because I now have a solid *why*. I no longer question what I am doing or why I am doing it. God has already determined it for me.

I have one purpose, and I am making that my mission.

— Kenajawa LaShawn

Say Aloud: **I Have One Purpose**

January 30

I Will Fill My Soul

One of the most irresistible urges our body has is thirst. We can all identify with the deep, innate longing to have our thirst quenched. It is a physiological necessity that cells are hydrated. We need water to live.

Our souls also have an insatiable longing to belong, to love and be loved, to be accepted, to give of ourselves to a purpose bigger than ourselves and our lives. the way to satisfy our innermost craving is to be filled with what truly brings refreshing and satisfaction; to reconnect to our soul's Creator and the purpose of the soul's existence. This purpose is serving, loving, and encouraging, building ourselves as we build others.

We were created in a community of relationship for relationship, even introverts, so, Yes, I will fill my thirsty soul with Living Water, exploring, loving and being loved, providing service to myself and others in the great exchange where I give life every day that I receive it. Every day, I refuse to give away without first replenishing the love tank of my supply.

— Dr. Latisha D. Reeves Henry

Say Aloud: **I Will Fill My Soul**

January

" All is Well with My Soul "

Let's be truthful. Stuff happens! I mean some *real* stuff!!! Some deep, dark, painful, sad... STUFF! When those dark times come, it can seem as if nothing is going right. It can seem as if sunny days will never return, but there is a place within us where no darkness can ever penetrate: This place is our soul.

Our soul is our most pure place. It is the place where we find our strongest connection to our source. It is our physical body and mind that are fragile, but our soul is the place from which we draw our strength. Our soul is the place from which we bring forth the wisdom required to successfully navigate during our time here on earth.

So, the next time things get difficult and dark clouds start to loom, although you may not be able to say, "All is well." You will always be able to say, "All is well with my soul." *...and that is more important than anything else that's going on.*

— Kwanza Yates

Say Aloud: **All is Well with My Soul**

Spirit!

February 1

> ## My JOY Comes in the Morning...
> ## EVERY Morning!!!

Life is a journey, and what we find on our road is not optional. However, how we handle our discoveries of life is optional. Like making lemonade out of lemons, sweet pies out of mud pies, and diamonds out of dirt... YES! These are some options of choices made on our journey through life.

Choose your course of life and choose to allow joy to reside in your soul despite all your experiences. Making a fragrant oil out of your tears is the path to waking up happy every day!

Therefore, having been justified by faith,
we have peace with God
through our Lord Jesus Christ.

Romans 5:1

— Carolyn E. Thompson

February 2

> ## I Will Rejuvenate My Spirit

Are you tired or overwhelmed by all your responsibilities? Are there not enough hours in the day? Is that project you committed to lasting much longer than you thought?

Have you seen your loved ones recently? Are you struggling to remember your *name*, and what's really important to you?

STOP! **STOP!** Stop and smell the roses.

Stop and make an appointment with yourself, for yourself, and *give* yourself permission to enjoy the things surrounding you. Taste and see that the Lord is good and the gifts He has given you are to be enjoyed: Family. Friends. Solitude. A bath. A movie. Shopping. Breath...

Breathe deeply and let the air rejuvenate your spirit.

— Mommy V

February

"Life is Only as Fun as I Imagine It to Be"

A lesson I've had to learn recently is that adulthood hits you fast. Once you enter the "real world," it is completely up to you to create a path for yourself. Your decisions will have a direct impact on your life—either in a positive or negative way.

As an adult, you can guide the direction you would like your life to take. And if you have the ability to guide your life, why not make life an amazing adventure? with the power to make your own decisions, you can choose to have fun. You can choose to travel, meet new people, try new things, grow as a person, and much more.

Dream big, and never say never. the person you are today is not the person you will be in ten years. Each year, we grow and change as individuals. You may think a dream you have today is too big, but it may be the perfect fit in five or ten years. Continue to challenge yourself and set goals. Live life to the fullest!

— Arielle Griffin

February

I Vow to Always Try New Things

Throughout life, continue to try new types of food, unique styles of clothing, hairstyles, etc. Attempting new things allows us to grow as women. It allows for less judgment of others and for our minds to remain open. Being set in our ways causes us to remain stagnant when we do not allow room for growth.

I am a huge advocate for trying various kinds of food. Learning about other cultures and their cuisine is so instrumental to our development as women. When I was younger, I would say, "I don't like that," when I had never tried a particular meal before. I was told to try the food I claimed not to like because I may surprise myself. Sometimes, I did surprise myself, and I enjoyed the food. Other times, I did not. However, at least I tried the food and could now say with complete confidence that I did not like it.

Always try new things. Do not limit yourself due to prior misconceptions. Wouldn't life be boring if we continued to eat the same foods, wear the same styles, or listen to the same music forever? You may surprise yourself.

— Arielle Griffin

Affirmation Journal

★ What are some things in my life that I have not yet tried?
★ What 2 new things can I try out *this* month?
★ What 2 new things can I try out *next* month?
★ What has kept me from trying new things in the past?
★ How will I vow to keep trying new things going forward?

February 5

I Will Travel

Traveling has been an important aspect of my life for as long as I can remember. It was very important for my mother that we see more than just the city in which we resided. She wanted us to have the opportunity to experience more of the world.

I can still remember the first plane ride I took. I was ten years old and was traveling with my aunt, uncle, and cousin. We traveled to Miami, Florida, to visit with another aunt who was living there at the time. It was such a wonderful trip. in addition to this trip to Miami, my family took many road trips when I was younger. We traveled to Tennessee, Georgia, South Dakota, the Carolinas, and much more. There was nothing quite like being woken in the middle of the night to travel to a surprise destination, fall asleep in the car, and to have arrived by the time I woke up again.

Even now, in my 20s, I still travel with family, but I have also taken many trips with friends. One of my future goals will be to travel miles away to a different state, or even to a different country alone. Spending time alone is so instrumental. I believe it will be fun to travel alone and to maybe even figure out the details along the way.

The best advice I can give anyone is to travel! See the world and expand your mind, no matter how young or how old you are!

— Arielle Griffin

Say Aloud: **I Will Travel**

February

"

I Will Take LOTS of Pictures

I have about 40,000 photos and videos saved to my computer right now. If there is one aspect of life I have defined as important, it is taking photos. This proved to be especially important during my college experience.

Looking back at the endless memories brings along old feelings and reminiscing. I am certain that if I did not take as many pictures as I did, I would most likely not remember many of the activities I participated in, the events I attended, or the random times I was hanging around with family acting silly.

Now that college is over, I take fewer "selfies." I still try to make a point to take photos daily. There is no better feeling than looking back at photos from months or years ago and remembering the feeling of that moment. It's bittersweet.

I am presently in a relationship that requires long-distance communication for extensive periods of time, so photos are even more important. Looking back at photos of good times is so helpful when we're apart.

When I decide to look back on photos and videos my parents took of me as a child, I am very grateful. I love to look back at the experiences and family members that were captured in those moments of time. This causes me to have the desire to take just as many photos when I have children of my own. I want my children to be able to have those same memories of life when they grow up.

— Arielle Griffin

Say Aloud: **I Will Take LOTS of Pictures**

February 7

Cherish Every Moment

Slow Down!

We can find ourselves moving through life at a very fast pace. the days go by fast. the months go by fast, and before we know it, the year is coming to an end. When is the last time you set aside time to cherish any moment?

Life progresses so fast because we are living our lives on a schedule—a busy schedule. Most of our days are consumed with the same things: work, school, church, hobbies. How many moments in our busy schedule do we truly cherish? Do you cherish the ride to work every morning? Do you cherish the conversations you have with friends, family or even a stranger in line at the grocery store? Do you cherish the blessings you have each day? Take this moment to stop and cherish what's happening right now.

If you ever feel like your life isn't worth much, it could be because you are comparing your life to someone else. Maybe you just feel like you can't enjoy the life you have because it's not good enough. Take some time to cherish what you have in your hands at this exact moment.

Cherish the moment, so you don't miss the moment.

— Kenajawa LaShawn

This Woman's Work (Always)

★ **In your time with family, friends, *and yourself*, remove all devices. Encourage others to do the same.**

February

I Will SHINE

Always shine in everything you do. Don't allow others to dull your happiness or positivity. with everything going on in this world, it can be easy to fall victim to the negativity. Shine when it comes to your attitude, but also shine when it comes to activities you participate in daily. This can include grocery shopping, helping the kids with homework, interactions with your family, and much more.

> People are much more willing to help you or be there for you if you exert a positive attitude or positive energy.

Shine at work, even when you don't necessarily feel like it. Others notice your demeanor even if you don't think they do. Have you been assigned to create a presentation? SHINE. Don't allow fear to hold you back and always continue to push forward. Be the best version of yourself you can be. You're allowed to have those days where you just feel "bleh," but always make a comeback. It will be so worth it. You are worth it.

Your best life is ahead of you, so Shine! Girl, SHINE!

— Arielle Griffin

Say Aloud: **I Will SHINE! I Will Live My BEST Life!!!**

February

"

I Will Shine Bright

"

We walk around with a light—not in hand, but in the heart. Has someone ever said, "There's just something about you," or "You are truly one of a kind."? They are speaking of the light you possess on the inside. It draws them to you. Shining from the inside out is the purest form of light. Your internal light is a light that cannot be replicated.

You are a gift to many, and even if you are a woman who says little, your presence is simply enough. Always remember no one can take your light from you unless you freely give it away. Fight for your light, for it is the thing that makes you uniquely you. It's not about hair, clothes, or where you live because that's not what makes you uniquely you. It's about authenticity and being genuine in your life.

In the next situation or circumstance you encounter, I want you to remember your light. Remember the goodness in *you*. Shine so bright that the next woman says, "I want just a little bit of whatever you've got!"

Shine bright like a diamond!

— Chantell Williams

Affirmation Journal
  * ★ How have I dimmed my light in the past?
  * ★ How have I allowed others to dim my light in the past?
  * ★ How can I be sure to let my light shine continually?
  * ★ Who will hold me accountable to this?

Say Aloud: I Will Shine Bright

I Will Always Start My Day with A Positive Attitude

If your day is filled with routine, it can be easy to start the day with a negative attitude—especially if it's a Monday. One thing that I have begun to practice recently is waking up with a positive attitude. I like to wake up and spend a few minutes in meditation, just relaxing before the hustle and bustle of the day. I tell myself, "Today will be a good day."

I have learned that if you speak positive words from your lips, this has a direct correlation to how the progression of your day goes. of course, things happen. Someone might be short with you in conversation at work, or you may spill coffee or yourself. However, the important thing is how you react to such events. If someone is short with you in conversation, they could be going through personal issues that have nothing to do with you. It is important to realize this and brush trivial things off. If you spill coffee on yourself, try to get the stain out, but understand that things happen. You have no choice but to continue your day—you might as well do so with a positive attitude.

Try not to waste your days by being unnecessarily upset or angry. Life is too short.

Cherish it.

—— Arielle Griffin

Say Aloud: I Will Always Start My Day Positively

February 11

"

Lessons Are Blessings

Everything we go through in life will be a lesson. You will either pass, or you will fail, but it's up to you to learn from the outcome—no matter what it is. Don't allow your trials to make you bitter, but rather, allow them to make you better!

Everything in life is a lesson; learn from them and move on. Shift happens to all of us. Make the necessary shift and remain focused on the ultimate goal.

Lessons are a blessing.

Don't forget to learn from them.

— Erika Harp

February 12

I Am Thankful

Thankfulness is an expression of gratitude and relief. I like this definition because both gratitude and relief affect our mental and emotional wellbeing. Gratitude helps us focus on what we have rather than what we don't have. Continuously giving thanks can remind us of the blessing rather than the desire, which in turn makes us happier. the more gratitude in our hearts, the more pleasant we are to others. the sense of relief at very crucial times can cause a stronger emotional response from us when it comes to our thankfulness.

This Woman's Work (Today)

★ **Think back at a time when you really needed something to come through in your favor.** It could have been a prayer to receive much-needed money at the last minute to pay a bill or a prayer to receive a positive test result from your physician.

★ **Write down 10 things that you're thankful for.**
★ **As you're writing, think about times of relief as well.**

Look at your list whenever you're having a bad day and compare your blessings with your desires.

— Cortney D. Surrency, AC-CHC

February 13

" I Thank, Therefore, I Am "

Are you busy thinking, or are you busy thanking?

We all know how the original version of this goes, "I think. Therefore, I am," or "As a man thinketh, so shall he be." That is true because the first part is thinking, but we must take things one step further. We must move past the desire to be, the desire to achieve, and the desire to obtain more. We must embark on a journey to maintain a continuous mind frame of thankfulness.

When we are thankful, we are asking the universe to give us more of the things we are thankful about. When we are thankful, we widen and strengthen the channel that flows blessings to us. When we are thankful, we are telling God we have faith in His plan and are committed to His will for our life, so if you are blessed and highly favored, be thankful.

— Kwanza Yates

February 14

I, and Only I, Am in Control of My Happiness!

You, and only you, are in control of your happiness. No outside person, place, or thing can MAKE *you* happy. So often we think, "If only I had this job, this house, this amount of money, this woman or man...,"—or fill in the blank with something else materialistic *(outside component)*—"then I'll be happy and fulfilled." These things can certainly make us feel good in the moment. But if we're not truly happy with who we *really* are... then we will subconsciously sabotage that job, misuse the money, or be a horrible mate to that man or woman. You see... the rich and well off *still* struggle with drugs, suicide, *and* they're always in therapy!!! *Money is not always the ultimate life fixer!*

Take a mirror. Look at yourself long and hard, and repeat, "Only I can make me truly happy!" Most importantly, remember this: what the next person thinks of you is none of your business. You're not living for them, and they are certainly not living for you!

— Monique Carter

Affirmation Journal

★ How have I allowed others to lead my happiness?
★ How can I take control of my own happiness?
★ What procedures will I use to commit to this?

"

I Will Face My Fears

"

Fear, dread, and anxiety can be paralyzing. They can rob us of our future or our intended destiny. Fear will cause us to settle into comfortable settings and forfeit greatness.

It would be a lie to say that life does not present us with things that cause fear. We are human. Fear, dread, and anxiety are a reality, but my advice to each of us is to stay determined to do it afraid. Face LIFE while you're scared!

There are many biblical characters who were afraid when they were called to great exploits: Moses, Joshua, Esther, Elijah, Mary, and Peter, to name a few. Joshua chapter one reveals that God tells Joshua repeatedly, "Do not be afraid," in a situation where He clearly ought to be afraid.

Why would God do that? I believe we are not called, not to deny fear, but to face fear in order to overcome it. Moses had to stand up to lead when He was petrified. Joshua had to face enemies that He feared in order to defeat them. Esther had to take ownership of her position in the palace so she could live in her power for the right time to save her people. Elijah had to face Jezebel and hundreds of false prophets to stand for the true and living God under the threat of death and the weight of depression. Mary surrendered to become the mother of the Savior of the world as a confused and frightened young girl. Peter, after denying Christ three times in fear, made up his mind to follow the teachings of Christ wholeheartedly. He went on to proclaim those same teachings boldly amidst persecution.

The encouragement and assurance each of these people had was not because they stopped being afraid. They found courage in doing what they were called to do in spite of fear. the beauty for them and us is the enduring promise that God is with us always, so ladies... it is time to face the fears.

— Dr. Latisha D. Reeves Henry

Say Aloud: I Will Face My Fears

" I Make the BEST of Even the Hardest of Times "

They say you're always either in the middle of a storm, walking into a storm, or coming out of a storm. This applies to everyone; no one is exempt. Hard times come at us while we simply mind our adulthood, our relationships, careers, finances, our families, and our health. Hardship is unpredictable and is not at all prejudiced to anyone. Eventually, as you go through hard times, you soon come to understand life's way of building your physical and mental muscles through waking us up or slowing us down and forcing us to appreciate all that's going right. We learn to be less judgmental and more sympathetic.

The next time you fall on hard times, pray—*ask* for guidance, and welcome the help with courage. Put on some coffee or hot tea. Grab a pen and paper, and then get to work. Consider how you were able to make it last time or how someone else you know surpassed something similar. Who would be a great person to confide in or ask for advice or to coach you through it even? Or, if you prefer, sit with your problem alone; sometimes, silence brings clarity. Hard times require research. Gather new tools and resources that are applicable to the situation. Ultimately, do whatever you have to do to create a sharper *you*.

After you've done all that, create a plan and work towards it with small action steps or by taking one big leap. Either way, you'll come out polished, wiser, and ready to take on another day... *or another hard time*. Only this time, you're better equipped. This is how we make the best of even the hardest times.

— Monique Carter

Say Aloud: **I Make the BEST of the Hardest Times**

17

February

I Am Courageous

I Am Courageous!
Having courage is to not be discouraged.
Courage provides the action behind your thoughts.
Courage is not daunted by danger; *courage protects!*
Courage is not daunted by pain; *courage praises!*
Courage is not daunted by lack; *courage thrives!*
Courage is not daunted by void; *courage makes whole!*
Life's toughest obstacles call for you to be courageous in ways you
didn't know existed. Stretch those muscles of faith and hope.
Be courageous!

— Regina N Roberts

18

February

I Will Speak Up!!!!

I Will Speak Up
I will speak up for what I believe in and speak up for what I know
is RIGHT! I will speak up for equality for all mankind. I will speak up
for those who have been robbed of their rights to live a life of
FREEDOM. I will speak up in times of sorrow and shame for others. I
will speak up for my family and my friends, my children, my nation,
my community, and my city.

I will speak up, so my voice is heard.

I will speak up in times of triumph and during hardship. I will speak
up to educate, empower, and enrich those around me. I will speak up

even when others aren't listening. I will speak up in ways that will compel others to speak up for themselves!

I will speak up to free myself from the bondage of shame and silence.

I Will Speak UP!!!!!!

— Regina N Roberts

February

I Will Stop Looking for Happiness in the Same Place I Lost It

Happiness can be orgasmic, and most of us know that... well... ummmm... that FEELS GOOD!

I have looked for happiness in sooooooo many places: Food. Sex. Work. Dating. Friends. Working Out. Money. Drinking... and yes, even in smoking *(earth's flowers)*.

None of these things is bad *(that is my opinion, which is relative)*. However, when you eat everything you see; date and sex every person who crosses your path; invest every free minute into the gym; trade all your time for dollars; search for happiness solely in friends; and consume mind-altering substances, it might be time to re-evaluate your life. *I'm just saying!*

Be mindful of the things you allow into your life that you think will bring you happiness. When you allow something the power to give you happiness, you are also giving that *something* power to **control** your happiness as well.

Affirmation Journal

★ What things am I giving power to control my happiness?

— Erika Harp

Say Aloud: **I Will Look for Happiness in New Places**

February

"

There's No Such Thing as Problems.
There are Only Challenges with Opportunities.

"

Problems, challenges, and opportunities are all based on your view of them. If you find them to be difficult, learn to change your view. Many times, the problems and opportunities aren't even difficult; they are just new to you.

Learn to look at new as *different*, rather than difficult. There's no such thing as problems. There are only challenges with opportunities. Look at them with a new view.

— Erika Harp

February

"

I Will Do That Which Scares Me Most

"

I will do that which scares me the most!

Standing here with you, fear, is no longer serving me. You have never served me to be honest. You have had me in bondage, in the dark and confused, yet oddly, I felt safe.

No more will I allow you, fear, to have power over me. I will study you and look within myself to see why I continue my life with you walking along my side. I will destroy you, fear, from the inside out. Then, I will take a deep breath and LEAP! I will do that which scares me the most!!!

Now, look at that! I landed on the other side and found assurance. on the other side of you, fear, I have found strength, adventure, knowledge, and elevation! YES! Now, this feels amazing! I am stronger, and I know my God has got me!!! the universe is on my side.

Standing up to you, fear, is now my adrenaline rush. I can't wait 'til the next thing I "fear" comes along. Again... I will take a deep breath... step to it... go through it... and come out better than when I went in.

Just the thought of no longer being afraid, and knowing I can conquer my BIGGEST fears, is the ultimate freedom!

— Monique Carter

Say Aloud: **I Will Do That Which Scares Me Most**

February
22

" I Will Show the WORLD Who I AM! "

I am spunky!

I am full of spice!

I will go after everything that I am called to do, and I will NOT let anything deter me. I will stay on my course, and I will finish this race. I will always believe that I can be great no matter what life throws, and no matter what I see. I will take life by its throat! I won't allow another opportunity to slip through my fingers!

I will show the world who I am!!!

I will show the world who God created me to be no matter what it takes, and no matter what I have to do. No matter who I have to let go, no matter what I have to leave, I will be what God has created me to be!

Using all that He has given me, I will show the world who I am!!! I am now ready!

— Coach Latoya Kight

Say Aloud: **I Will Show the WORLD Who I AM!**

I Am Highly Favored!

I am highly favored. Favor is fair because God is fair. God favors me even in my lack. God favors me even in my mess. God favors me even when I'm not worthy enough. God favors me even when I don't do Him right all the time. God favors me because I am His child!

I AM Highly Favored! I am blessed beyond measure. the mere fact that God thinks about me out of all the people in the world lets me know that I mean something to Him. He will come and see about me and make sure I'm taken care of is astonishing in itself! I thank God for all the favor that has been bestowed upon my life! I thank God for positioning me to receive the favor He has for me! Why does God see fit to bless certain people? That's the amazing mystery of God. It is ALL in His timing! It's ALL at His discretion. He moves like no other. He pours out blessings upon us all, and as He pours out, I receive ALL that I can because, as long as He favors me, I will ALWAYS know... I am HIGHLY favored!

— Coach Latoya Kight

I Refuse to Be Ordinary!

To be ordinary is to "fit in," be normal, and be basic. Because of my self-worth, I REFUSE to be normal. I am MORE than a standard!

We don't pick our family; Generational trends and traits are hereditary, yet through self-discovery, self-love, and growth, we set the course for the lives we ultimately lead.

Therefore, I refuse to be ordinary. I refuse to allow ordinary things in this life to penetrate my physical, mental, and emotional well-being. Despite what society projects, I refuse to live a life that is predetermined by societal trends or generational models. I refuse to walk a path on the road most traveled. I accept the fact that I am—and will be—different. I refuse the ordinary and will instead flourish in the extraordinary! I refuse to be ordinary and will confront challenges, pain, disappointment, lack, and face the unknown in extraordinary ways.

Ordinary people believe only in the possible.

Extraordinary people visualize not what is possible or probable, but what is impossible.

> *And by visualizing the impossible,*
> *they begin to see it as possible.*
>
> Cherie Carter-Scott

— Regina N Roberts

February 25

I Am One Day Closer to My Deliverance!

Before reading this, review Jeremiah 52:31-34.

What would you do today if you knew that everything about your life would be changed by this time tomorrow? I am not talking dying. What if you gave up today, yet tomorrow was the day that God had predestined for your deliverance?

So many people commit suicide—spiritually and naturally—because they see no hope of a better day. Jesus Christ is the same—yesterday, today, and forever more. If He has delivered others, He can deliver you. God rains on the just and the unjust. God is a God of mercy. God delivered Jehoiachin from prison when all hope for deliverance was gone.[1] Have you stopped hoping for your deliverance? Have you aborted your dream?

---

[1] Jeremiah 52:31-34

My words to you are these:

You Are ONE DAY Closer to DELIVERANCE!

Don't give up!
By this time tomorrow, everything could change. God is a God of "suddenly!" He can use what He wills, how He wills, when He wills it! Nothing is impossible for God. You have come this far.
Don't quit now.

— Freda Wells

February

My Journey is a Marathon, Not A Sprint

It's imperative that you *over*stand that your life journey is a process. Remain patient. Treat your journey as a marathon and not as a sprint. In this marathon of life, it's important to set your own pace. Remember to breathe. And finish the race.

Progress is a process. As long as you are moving forward, you will win. FORWARD MOVEMENT! That's that goal!

Sometimes, people mistake being busy as being productive. If your movement equates to you doing figure 8's *(going in circles, with no forward movement)*, that process is **not** productive. We need forward movement—not figure 8's.

The process is what helps to build your character and to mold you into exactly who you are meant to become.

Take time with your process.

Your journey takes time.

— Erika Harp

Live Fully.
Die Empty.

The dash between birth and death is small, yet it holds the stories of a lifetime. So often, people are waiting to make their *next move*. Why? If there is something YOU want to do, then why are YOU not doing it? Don't wait until what happens *next* for you—start NOW! Live your life fully NOW! Start that business! Go on that vacation! Apply for that position! And write that book!

WHATEVER IT IS YOU WANT to DO…

GO, DO IT!

Live fully and die empty, having given your life **fully** to accomplishing WHAT **YOU** WANT to DO!!

Live fully.

Die having done all the very BEST you could have done to live the very BEST life that you could have lived.

Die empty.

— Erika Harp

Affirmation Journal

★ What does it mean to live life fully?
★ Who are some examples of living a full life?
★ What can I learn from them?
★ What can I do to be sure that I live my life FULLY?
★ How can I die empty?

Say Aloud: **I Will Live Fully. I Will Die Empty.**

Dance Like Nobody's Watching

Dance like nobody's watching.

What does that mean?

For me, the act of dancing has been something I've enjoyed since I was a child. As I grow older, dancing gives me a sense of celebration, love, and warmth in my spirit, soul, and body.

For many people, dancing tells a story. It is used as a form of exercising and as a symbol of celebration and worship. Dancing is also used in many cultural traditions and festivities to demonstrate honor, community, and delight!

As you evolve, you learn to adopt a dance of your own that signifies love, life, and legacy. It is a dance that praises every accomplishment and heals every pain. Don't wait for others to acknowledge your growth, accomplishments, and failures. Learn to acknowledge all you've learned and given life through your own dance!

Don't worry about who's watching or if you are making the right move and moving at the right tempo. Just Dance! Dance in a way that heals your soul. Dance in a way that clears your heart and mind from clutter. Dance until your heart beats faster and the blood in your veins gets warmer. Create your own purpose to dance. Create your own tempo—your own rhythm. Dance like nobody's watching!!!

— Regina N Roberts

Say Aloud: I Will Dance Like Nobody's Watching

A Newfound Spirit Has Awakened Within Me

Life's ups and downs can be devastating at times. We find that we cannot control what may happen to us, and we may feel helpless and hopeless. As a person who has experienced breast cancer *(stage zero)*, and lymphatic cancer *(stage three)*, I have learned—through prayer and the encouragement of others—what love looks and feels like.

Life really is fragile. Life is amazing. A newfound spirit has now awakened within me. God never readied me to come home. He did, however, ready me to see and feel differently spiritually.

God says,

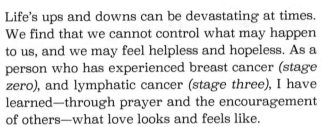

"In the beginning,
I created the heaven
and the earth."

He created all things beautiful, so that we who have second and third and many more chances, can see His works.

His beauty.
His love.

— MommyV

Say Aloud: A New Spirit Has Awakened Within Me

Mind!

March 1

"

I Will Meditate to Clear My Mind.
I Will Meditate for Peace!

"

Meditation has many wellness benefits, and my wellness is top priority! How peaceful is it to clear your mind of thoughts, breathe deeply, and relax? Meditating reduces stress, increases focus, calms chatter, reduces memory loss, enlightens, and melts away aggravation *and pettiness too!* This practice allows you to break bad habits, grow spiritually, and let go of limiting beliefs.

Meditation requires stillness! Most of us are not practicing being still nearly enough, and it shows. It shows in our lack of judgment, quick anger, and when we make mistakes.

Let's take a moment to talk about self-control. Life can throw the unexpected at us—we simply react and respond. Meditating will improve your self-control by increasing your mental power and clarity. We react rationally when we're in control of our thoughts.

Now, I want you to put this into practice:

* ★ Find a quiet place.
* ★ Sit or lie down.
* ★ Take a few deep breaths.
* ★ Some find it calming to chant a word repeatedly or speak affirmations.
* ★ You can look up videos of guided meditation on everything from stress relief, healing, anxiety, to clearing negativity.
* ★ Take a few moments to do this daily, even if only for several minutes.

You owe it to yourself. You owe it to your peace!

— Monique Carter

March 2

"I Will Heal My Mind"

How do you heal the mind? Meditation—that's how!

Meditation compliments all faith practices because it is tailored to your beliefs. It has been said that praying is when you talk to God and meditation is when you listen God. Neuroplasticity is the brain's ability to reorganize itself by forming new neural connections. in less scientific terms, neuroplasticity is the brain's ability to heal itself and create new nerve cells. This process compensates for injury and disease by adjusting the nerve cells to new activities throughout life. Meditation is one avenue to healing the mind after injury, disease, or dis-ease! There are different forms of meditation including mindfulness or guided meditation. for beginners, I recommend silent meditation as sometimes it is best to be still, be simple, and be silent. This type of meditation is easy to do and doesn't take a lot of time for a person to receive the benefits.

Here are some tips to begin your regular meditation:

* Start meditating once daily for 15-20 minutes.
* Don't judge yourself.
* Use a mantra (a focus word or sentence) of your choice to stay focused. Maranatha is an Aramaic word that means, "Lord, come."

★ Use any mantra you like. Try using something that won't make you think.

The goal is to rest the mind. When distractions come—and they will—say your word to refocus yourself.

Say it with me...

Ma-Ra-Na-Tha.

— Cortney D. Surreney, AC-CHC

- -

March

It Will Be Worth It.
I Will Keep My Mind on Track.

If there is something you desire to accomplish, it is important to stay focused. Keep your mind on track and your eyes on the prize. It can be easy to become distracted, as sometimes, we may become bored with our goals or may not be as motivated to achieve them as we once were.

Following through with your tasks can be so rewarding. in the end, you will be happy that you decided to stay focused. You will have completed something important to you.

Distractions appear in many areas of life. Choose to limit distractions at work, when spending time with family, and when having conversations. Live in the moment. Choose not to be distracted. It will be worth your while.

— Arielle Griffin

March 4

I Will LISTEN to My INSTINCTS

Your gut is smarter than you think. That gut feeling you ignore could be saving you some trouble and heartache, but we continuously ignore this primal survival instinct. Whether it is in business or personal relationships, as we move throughout our daily activities, your body will give you clues on how you should react to a situation. Listen to it.

Before making your next major decision, take a step back, and listen to what that gut feeling it trying to relay to you. You are more capable than you give yourself credit for. Just listen to your instincts and move forward.

— Brittany Whigham

March 5

I Will Never Stop Believing in Myself

Before reading this, review Mark 9:23.

You can't accidentally become who you desire to be. YOU must BELIEVE in yourself...

...your abilities...

...your dreams...

...and all that encompasses YOU.

You must STRONGLY believe in who you desire to become.
If you don't believe in yourself...
         ...then you're lying to yourself...
                  ...and lying to yourself is worse!
   YOU are the worst person for YOU to lie to. *(My grandma says so, so it's a FACT!).*
   Believe in yourself...
   ...believe in what you desire to accomplish.
   Believe in who you desire to become.

— Erika Harp

6
March

" I Will Eliminate Distractions! "

I will eliminate distractions such as useless chatter, random TV scrolling, and all that smartphones give us access to. I will eliminate mindless social media scrolling. Social media can distract you from what's truly important, bring on envy when everyone is posting about how "great" their lives are, and frankly, it can be a waste of time. It can also impact you emotionally, as you're internalizing everything you see and read. Give it a break altogether or simply cut back.

Stop spending useless time gossiping about what others are doing with their lives *(in person or over the phone)*. Say *NO* to some of the invites you receive and be okay with it. We cannot be everywhere for everybody all the time; we cannot be everything for everybody. Shut the electronics off for a while. Fill this time doing whatever it is that you say you have no time to do... You know—read that book, finish that workout, spend playtime with your kids, help them learn, or cook a nice meal. Mommies, prepare yourself and the family for the next day *completely*, so your morning runs smoother. Take a few minutes of personal time each evening—turn off the TV and computer and put your phone away. Replace this time with something intimate, something that will edify your soul and your household.

— Monique Carter

March

" My Success and Failure Starts with a Thought "

Success or failure in life starts first with a thought. Thoughts determine success or failure because we can convince ourselves of anything based upon what we think. We can also change the course of our life based on what we think.

Every good invention and every groundbreaking discovery began with just a thought. An African American woman named Gladys Mae West was very instrumental in the creation of what we now know as the Global Positioning System or the GPS. It started as a thought and has revolutionized life as we now know it. the same goes for you. That one thought could be what changes the world to come. Your thoughts are so powerful. Your next thought could be the next greatest invention. Your next thought could be the next groundbreaking discovery. You can change the course of your day by one thought negative thoughts, so daily start to focus on the positive. You have the ability to think positive about any situation. Your thoughts about a situation change the outcome of the situation. Nelson Mandela changed the way I look at think at situations by a quote, which was one of his thoughts. the quote says, "I never lose; I either win or learn." Thinking that way takes failure out of the equation. Because if you learned the lesson, it wasn't a failure, it was a lesson. So, mind your thoughts. Philippians 4:8 "8 Finally, brethren, whatsoever things are true, whatsoever things are honest, whatsoever things are just, whatsoever things are pure, whatsoever things are lovely, whatsoever things are of good report; if there be any virtue, and if there be any praise, think on these things.

— Coach Mechelle Canady

Say Aloud: **My Success Starts with a Thought**

March

"

I Have MUCH That I Desire to ACCOMPLISH, And I Will Accomplish ALL That I Set My Mind to Pursue.

"

I have much that I desire to accomplish. Complacency does not look good on me. There's something deeply inspiring about the intense fire and passion that comes with having a dream, goals, and the overall pursuit of it all. We are here on borrowed time, and one day, we will be someone to read about in history, so why not live out loud and dream big?! One day soon, your impactful achievements and accomplishments will be your legacy.

I am not here on this beautiful earth by chance. I have a meaningful purpose. There is a reason my desires keep me wide-eyed and up at night, then wake me bright and early in the morning. My dreams are more significant than sleep. They overpower mindless activities. My time is used intentionally, with intense focus, starving all distractions. I will visualize these accomplishments as if they've already come to fruition. I will lay out a plan to succeed and follow this plan with prayer and hard work. I will wake up each day and push toward these desires until completion.

— Monique Carter

This Woman's Work (This Week)

- ★ **List 3 goals that you aim to finish by the end of the year.**
- ★ **Spend 5 mins meditating on each one.** Consider what life looks like with that accomplishment. What changes? What improves? How do people respond to you now? What's next?
- ★ **This should take you a total of 15 mins.**
- ★ **Finally, write down a 5-10 step plan under each goal.** Spend a few minutes each day working your plan.

My Skills Are Powerful!

I hold within me the power to change the world! We were all created for a special purpose, and the skills that we already have inside of us is all that we need. But if we are honest, we don't believe in ourselves enough to believe in our power. I challenge you today to stop allowing people to control your power. Stop letting fear control your power! Stop letting insecurities control your power! Stop allowing your past to control your power! You are already equipped, but it's up to you to use your equipment.

What skills do you have inside of you already that you can use to access your power?

You must believe in every skill that you have, even the smallest ones. Something as simple as having a radiant smile is a skill that is powerful. with that skill, you are able to change the dynamic of a room. with that skill, you are able to change the course of someone's day, and you are able to bring light into a dark world. When you are feeling unimportant to the world, remember that your skills are powerful, and so are you.

Write down at least three skills to remind yourself that you are powerful!

— Kenajawa LaShawn

This Woman's Work (Today)

★ **Write down 3 skills of yours.**
★ **Under each skill, list 3 steps you will take to use the skill regularly.**
★ **Write a relevant affirmation next to each skill that will keep you encouraged.**

My WORDS Are POWERFUL

The words we speak are powerful. They are spirit and life. They are alive with the ability to activate and motivate. the opposite can also be true. Words that are overly critical, brash, and spoken with ill-will enter our psyche and live deeply embedded within our thought life. Without intervention, the result can make us stagnant, bitter, or unproductive in an unfulfilled life. We cannot afford to ignore the power of words. Instead of passively letting demise invade our territory, we choose divine proclamations of purpose, love, and grace toward ourselves. We must speak well of ourselves to ourselves about our lives, our loved ones, and our destiny.

It was words that were used to frame the world. They are building blocks to our thoughts which shape our actions. Words are seeds that produce a harvest. When affirming us, words fuel imagination, bring forth possibility, and cancel the assignment of curses birthed through careless loose lips.

Sticks and stones may break my bones, and yes, words can certainly hurt me, but my words are powerful when I gather them from the deepest well of inexhaustible truth and speak them to, over, and all around myself and my circumstances. Words build bridges to my better hope for the future, steadily killing the weeds that once tried to supplant them.

Speak your positive words of truth outwardly into this world until they cause life to live in and through you. Your words are powerful!

— Dr. Latisha D. Reeves Henry

Affirmation Journal

- ★ *What types of negative words am I using daily?*
- ★ *How will I increase the positivity in my words?*
- ★ *Who will I call now to hold me accountable?*

The Power to Change My Life Resides in Me

I contain the power to change my life
Everything I need is already within me
No person has as much control as me
No matter how much the trials of the world attempt to alter me
I Am Powerful
My life was considered before my parents even thought of me
I am worthy
I am important
I am chosen
I am enough
I Am Powerful

My life changed dramatically when I realized that everything I needed to live the life I wanted was already inside of me. Before deciding to publish my first book, I was stuck. I had just come out of a dark place in my life. I was confused about where I should go next in life. Then, I decided that I was not going to be stuck anymore. I told myself that from that point forward, I would do everything that I wanted. I didn't want to have any regrets. Even if I failed, I would be able to say, "At least I attempted it."

I took back my power and began to change my life. You can do the same!

Affirmation Journal

★ **How are you going to take back your power today?**

— Kenajawa LaShawn

There Is Power in Silence

I remember many years ago watching *I Know Why the Caged Bird Sings*. It was the story of young Maya Angelou. While the knowledge of her personal tragedy rocked me to the core, I have always been fascinated by what the world received, partly because of her years of silence.

Silence provides space to think, **meditate**, ponder, sort through and write, read, or record—it spurs creativity. Silence at the right time speaks loudly, declaring, "Peace! Be still." Silence is also the place where we listen and are able to hear clearly. Revelation comes through quieting noise. Journaling moves from a good idea to a reality. We hear the daily rhythms of life, our own heartbeat, and purpose because when we stop talking—admiring our voices—we finally hear God's.

— Dr. Latisha D. Reeves Henry

I Control the Negative Energy That Will Indeed Appear

Controlling negative energy is not about avoiding negative feelings and thoughts; those will come. You will feel bad sometimes, and you will have negative thoughts from time to time. When you try to ignore negativity altogether, that's when the danger occurs. Drinking, drugs, lashing out, engaging in excessive pornography or dangerous sexual behavior, retail therapy, overeating, and even self-mutilation are some manifestations of unrevealed and unhealed internal pain and suffering. After partaking in these negative and destructive actions, we feel bad all over again. Then, we have negative thoughts again, and the vicious cycle goes on and on.

When that next negative feeling occurs, put a halt to it, and immediately begin to think something different; think of something better. the goal is not to avoid the thoughts, but rather, the goal is for you to take control of the negative energy once it appears.

— Kwanza Yates

March

So That Life Doesn't Get the Best of Me, I Make Sure I Have A Firm Handle on *It*

To make sure life doesn't get the best of me, I stand firm in what I believe. I must go forth knowing that my standards cannot waver. I have to stay true to who I am and what I believe. If I don't, I will fall.

If I don't stay true to who I am, I will lose my mind. If I don't stay true to my beliefs, I will sink. If I don't stick to what I know is true, if I don't stick to what my standard is, and if I don't stay planted and grounded, then I know it would take me out!

I have to continue to go through life with my head held high come what may. If I allow situations and things that come my way to rise against me and take me out, then I won't accomplish what I'm supposed to accomplish. My dreams won't manifest if I quit, so I have to look beyond where I am right now. I have to believe that I am strong, and I am mighty. I have to believe I have the victory because of Christ.

Nothing can defeat me. Nothing can harm me. Nothing can get in my way unless I let it. I will stay firmly planted, like a tree.

— Coach Latoya Kight

March

I Will Do All I Can to Keep My Mental Space Healthy

I will protect my peace!
I will protect my sanity!
I will protect my mental health!

Your mental health is important; it is your life. for a long time, I did not realize how many things were actually affecting my mental health. I would hold on to relationships that I knew I needed to let go of. I found myself caring about the feelings of others more than I cared about my own. After seeking help, I realized how important it was to keep my mental space clear. I was no longer ashamed to cut off people who meant me no good. I no longer felt guilty about not doing things that others liked if I didn't like those things. I learned the value of saying no.

Affirmation Journal

★ **What can you do to keep your mental space healthy?**

Try these things:

★ **Find someone to talk to.**
It can be a professional or a trusted friend.

★ **Find your coping mechanisms.**
I love to journal to clear my head.

★ **Find your peace!**
My peace is God, so anytime I feel off-balance, I go to him.

★ **Find mental health accountability friends.**
These are people you can call when things are ugly. They don't only listen, but they help you out of that dark space and back into a healthy one!

— Kenajawa LaShawn

I Will Work to Heal Myself

When working on my undergraduate degree as a psychology major, I remember learning about the negative impact of suppressing painful memories. the consequences can be detrimental to one's emotional health and well-being. Suppressing means that we try to hide or bury the unpleasant things in life and chose only to acknowledge the good things.

Genesis 4 shows us a picture of what happens when we refuse to confront painful memories and disappointments. God speaks directly with Cain and tells him, "Sin is crouching at your door, but you must master this." Why? Because God knows that what is on the inside will come out. Both Cain and His brother Abel brought offerings to God. Abel's offering was acceptable to God, but Cain's offering was found to be unacceptable.

Cain murdered his brother, who had committed no wrong against him. Choosing not to be open before God and deal with the deep pain of what He wrongly thought was rejection or favoritism by God toward His brother cost Cain more than He ever intended to pay. He lost his brother and friend, the penalty of which was that He would be a vagabond without stability and the warmth of loving family connection for the rest of his life. His parents lost two sons. Cain also lost the place of His center of being: His home in the culture of community.

When we refuse to uncover and open up in order to rid ourselves of the stuff that keeps us bound, not only are we held hostage to the excruciating pain of the past, so are others in our lives. They suffer as we kill or abandon them based on what we have experienced.

Despite this, TODAY is the day of salvation. Today, we refuse to slaughter another sister or brother, another relationship, or friendship! As my girl says, "Honey! Go get your *whole* life back!" Let us affirm this as an absolute truth: I will not suppress painful memories. I will confront them to heal myself. I WILL MASTER THIS!

If it takes a therapist, wise counsel, kick-boxing, prayer retreats, treatment centers, or three girls' trips a year, GET BUSY. We have too much to do. the world is awaiting our arrival.

We've got this!

— Dr. Latisha D. Reeves Henry

March

My Strength is Renewed!

How are you feeling today? Are you feeling down or unmotivated today? It's time to get up! Every day will not be a good day, and your emotions may not always be positive, but you must do what it takes to renew your strength daily.

How do I renew my strength, you ask? the answer is simple: **God!**

My strength comes from him, and once I realized that, I then knew what I needed to do when I felt weak. Isaiah 40: 29 tells me, "He gives strength to the weary and increases the power of the weak," so when you feel weak, and you need strength, go to the ultimate power source. There is nothing that you can go through in life that God can't help you through. Depending on ourselves or others is not always viable, but God is. He is your strength.

Prayer:

God, thank you for all that you are doing for us today. We thank you for being the ultimate power source and for being here for us in every moment. Help us to remember, on days like today, that our power comes from you. Help us to remember that there is no problem too big for you. Thank you for giving us unconditional dependability. We love you, Father, and all these things we pray in your name. Amen!

— Kenajawa LaShawn

March 18

I Am Liberated

As a black woman, using the affirmation "I Am Liberated" feels so victorious! Most people relate being liberated to being free or to being a freethinker. I prefer not to use the term *freethinker*, nothing about your thinking is free. Your mind has the ability to think million-dollar thoughts, so you are not a freethinker!! A freethinker sounds like a novice in comparison to a person with a liberated mind. A liberated mind is mentally free. It is the mind of an independent thinker who has critical thinking skills.

Be liberated.

Free your mind!

— Erika Harp

March 19

I Will Expand My Knowledge Through Books

"I can't wait until I get out of school. I'm not reading another book!"

Those were my words often in school when the reading and workload felt overwhelming. At the time, I did not have a clue that I would develop a love of learning through reading and writing. I have learned that I love knowing more of what I did not know; reading helps me to know now what I do know.

Expanding your knowledge through books means stretching your understanding and perspective to see beyond what is immediately tangible, what is already known. Books provide a guide, a roadmap. They pique our interest and take us to distant lands long before we can purchase a ticket to go there. Books help increase our capacity to receive, to dream, and books inspire us to *be*. Books speak when spoken word cannot. They give us a glimpse into the past and light the pathway along the journey of our future. They comfort. They invite us into the future.

Take a journey, learn a skill, see a story in your mind's eye as you turn the pages of a favorite read. Expand your knowledge and unleash your imagination. Have a look in a book.

— Dr. Latisha D. Reeves Henry

20
March

I Will Never Stop Learning . . .

Every day brings a new opportunity to add one more chapter of knowledge to my mental *Great Book of Wisdom*. I look at it this way: everything I've learned up to this point is based on my past experiences through the people I've known, books I've read, places I've been, and movies or television shows I've watched. My beliefs, and my perspective on life, are based on my experiences.

There is so much to uncover. From the morning talks about history with the mature woman at the front desk, to the young and vibrant college students sprinkled throughout the office—they all teach me daily something new and something applicable to everyday life.

Take advantage of those little moments of time for personal growth and development. Listen to audio recordings of books, speeches, podcasts, read an article, travel, oar... take that class! Focus on what invites your genuine curiosity and dive in! You never know what jewels of wisdom you may find that will have a profound effect on your life.

— Monique Carter

March

" I Will Study to Show Myself Approved "

2 Timothy 2:15 reminds believers to consistently study to show themselves approved to God as workers who need not be ashamed but who rightly divide the word of truth.

I can remember thinking and hearing in error that this meant we must study to be approved. How thankful I am for growth, study, and learning the importance of understanding scripture in context. Paul was not instructing Timothy to study for God's approval. Paul was instructing Timothy to study because He was already approved, called, and set-aside by God for the work of leading others. He instructed that Timothy would be committed to study, to holy living rightly dividing, teaching, and proclaiming God's word without shame or reservation. It was a call to preparation, fortification, and to a faithful response born of love.

Sisters, let our declaration be that we will study to show ourselves approved as those chosen to do the great work of leading, mentoring, nurturing, birthing, and coaching others. I WILL study to show myself approved as a response of love for the One who issued the call, imparted the gifts, and keeps providing the opportunities. I study—not for approval—but because I am already approved! It is my response to the sacred call of preparation, fortification, and my personal faithful response born of love.

— Dr. Latisha D. Reeves Henry

This Woman's Work (Today)

★ *Take time to read 2 Timothy 2:15.*
★ *Rewrite the scripture in your own words.*
★ *Take note of the deeper meaning that you gather.*
★ *Put continual effort into studying to show yourself approved.*

I Am A Lifelong Learner

A lifelong learner is someone who has begun to understand and embrace the fullness of life. Living is connected to purpose. You exist to impact the world in some grand way, and that purpose for your life is the overarching goal and center of why and how you do what you do. As a lifelong learner, you know that learning is growth that brings expansion of days, influence, and fulfillment. If you are not learning, you are not growing. Learning happens when you open and avail yourself to take in and process information, to receive revelation, and to make application. the *result is transformation!*

Let's free ourselves to pursue what we do not know. These pursuits will make us better, give us life, energize our efforts, and teach us as we teach others. As we learn, we thrive with a proper perspective. We become conduits for hire to give what we get. Challenge yourself to rise to the occasion of learning.

Personally, I am a lifelong learner whose life is longer because of what I have gained. Learning has lengthened my days. Together, let us open ourselves to new and better, growth and change through learning, living, and passing it on.

— Dr. Latisha D. Reeves Henry

Affirmation Journal

* *Where in life have I slacked on learning?*
* *What do I lose in life if learning is not a focus?*
* *How will I get back into a focus on learning?*
* *How will I encourage others to do the same?*

Say Aloud: **I Am A Lifelong Learner**

March

Trust the Process

The Book of Jeremiah chapter 18 shows us the prophet Jeremiah at the potter's house observing the making of a useful clay vessel. It was a vessel forged by the hands of the master, then baked in the heat of a fiery furnace. Due to the direction of God's leading, the purpose for the prophet being sent there was so He might have a visual illustration of the message He was commissioned to speak to God's people: God is the Potter. His people are clay which the Potter can mold as it pleases Him. the same is still true.

The Potter does not see a lifeless lump as many others do when looking at the earthen substance of clay. the Potter sees the clay through the lens of its intended purpose. When the clay is marred, it must be broken, reshaped, molded, hardened, and perfected by fire. the suitability of the clay takes a discerning eye able to see even the slightest imperfections and foreign objects needing to be removed to prohibit future defects. the final product is a finished product aptly fit for the purpose for which it was created.

Trust the process—all the struggle and uncertainty are part of the making of a unique vessel greatly necessary for the Master's use.

He who has begun a good work in you is faithful to carry that work to completion until the day of Christ Jesus

Philippians 1:6

— Dr. Latisha D. Reeves Henry

Say Aloud: **I Will Trust the Process**

I Will Trust My Instincts

Trusting your instincts is so important, especially as a woman.

There have been a number of situations where I felt something was wrong, and I trusted my instincts. If something feels off, it probably is. When my instincts kick in, I think of this as God guiding me in the right direction. He's giving me a little nudge that may afford me the confidence to escape a potentially dangerous situation.

On the other hand, trusting your instincts can be the notion of leaving a toxic relationship or a thought on how to further your career.

The older I grow, the more I believe in women's intuition.

It's that feeling you get when you know what is right, but you just need to trust that you're making the right decision. More often than not, trusting your instincts will be beneficial in some way. Try not to overthink or second guess yourself. Trust yourself and trust your instincts.

— Arielle Griffin

Affirmation Journal

- ★ What does it mean to trust my instincts?
- ★ How do I feel when I trust my instincts?
- ★ What are the benefits of doing this regularly?
- ★ How can I practice doing this more often?

March

The Only Thing Worse than Fear
is Never Trying

A life of fear leads to a life of regret. Fully live your life!
Do you think Oprah was camera shy the first time?

Yes!

Do you think Steve Jobs' first presentation of software (*named after a piece of fruit*) led to his billion-dollar estate?

Probably not.

I'm sure they were nervous, anxious, scared, full of fear, but...
...they did it anyway and look at them now!
Don't let fear be the reason you fail.
The only thing worse than fear is never trying, so...
Just try.
Don't live to regret that you never did.

— Erika Harp

March

Timing is Everything.
Be Ready for Anything!

There are three things that leave and never return: words, time, and opportunities.

- ★ Your words have power, so be mindful of the words you speak. You can speak desires into existence as well into extinction.
- ★ Timing is everything. When the time comes, you BETTER be ready! the timing allows you to take advantage of opportunities.
- ★ Opportunities happen on purpose, so be sure that, when the time comes, you take advantage of the opportunity.

Words. Time. Opportunity.

Be ready when they come.

— Erika Harp

March

I Will Learn from My Past and Prepare for My Future

Yesterday is gone.

The best thing you can do is learn from it. What worked? What didn't work? How could it have been done, said, or experienced better?

The future has yet to come.

The best thing you can do is prepare for it. What will work? What won't work? How can it be done, said, or experienced in the best way possible?

What remains is the present—the ever-existing moments we live in—the most important moments of our lives. It is in these moments that we put forth our energy to create and to consume. Enlighten and Enjoy. Plan and Play. in these moments, we are given the opportunity to be our best, and when we are not our best, we can learn from our past and prepare for our future.

— Kwanza Yates

Say Aloud: **I Will Learn from Yesterday's Experience**

"I Will Stop and Smell the Roses. . . "

We are so busy! We rush from one thing to another and never truly take time to stop and smell the roses.

We go through life like it's the quick meal we grab during a 30-minute lunch break—a meal that took 20 minutes to prepare, so we only have a few minutes to inhale it before we rush back to work. We don't truly taste it. We barely smell it or even enjoy it for that matter. It's as though we're on a hamster wheel through life.

Take a moment to enjoy the fruits of your labor. Pause, if only for a moment, and evaluate where you truly are in life and how you feel about it. When you're headed out the door or coming in from a long day, be sure to give a loved one a heartfelt hug and kiss. Go for a walk and connect with nature, while breathing in some fresh air. Make it a point to do this daily.

Stop being too busy for the people that love you, and most importantly, stop being too busy to take properly take care of YOU!

— Monique Carter

Affirmation Journal

- ★ **Where are the busy areas in my life?**
- ★ **Where am I entirely *too* busy in life?**
- ★ **What is this busy-ness causing me to miss out on?**
- ★ **What opportunities do I have to slow?**
- ★ **How will slowing down help to ease my mind?**

Say Aloud: **I Will Stop and Smell the Roses. . .**

I Will Get Rest

Getting rest is a vital component to your physical, mental and emotional health. When the body and mind don't rest well, you are not able to live life effectively. I am sure you have lots of questions when it comes to the topic of rest, but for starters, let's just keep it simple. Here are some rest related tips to get you on the right track.

★ It's said that you need eight hours of sleep, but that varies by individual. You should go by how you feel at the end of the day. Some people need six and some need ten. the important thing is to be consistent.

★ Try to go to bed and wake up at the same time every day, even on the weekends! This helps your body recognize when it's time to go to bed and when it's time to wake up!

★ Keep your room dark and invest in comfortable sheets.

★ You should eat your last meal at least three hours before bedtime and stop use of all electronics at least 1 hour before bed.

★ Clearing of the mind is crucial to sleep. Don't have a difficult conversation or make a to-do list before bed because you will dream about it all night!

★ Read a good book or a do 5 to 10-minute meditation to clear your mind and begin relaxation before sleeping each night.

— Cortney D. Surrency, AC-CHC

I Will REST, RELAX and Reflect

Between our families, careers, businesses, health, and overall life management, we're constantly on the go. We are *indeed* super, but we're still human. Just like a battery runs low on power and needs charging or a car running out of gas needs refueling, we must take a moment to unplug. Allowing our bodies to rest will, in turn, increase our energy.

Rest allows the body to heal physically, mentally, and emotionally. Once you have personally made the decision to rest, truly relax; stop your mind from running a mile a minute, try meditation even. Focus on the moment of relaxation, feel your muscles relax, loosen tension in your jaws, your neck, and your shoulders, and breathe deeply. Then, reflect on all the things you have to be grateful for *(health, family, shelter, nourishment, and endless opportunities)*. Reflect on how much you've accomplished, how far you've come, and how much you've grown. Reflection also requires an honest evaluation of your true current state. Reflection, once you're relaxed, allows you to quiet your mind despite how noisy and busy it may be. Once your mind relaxes, then... slowly... cautiously... sort through the many piles of life's goings-on. This brings organization, and most importantly, peace of mind.

Rest. Relax. And Reflect.

— Monique Carter

This Woman's Work (Today)

- ★ **Create a list of 3-5 peaceful places in your city.**
- ★ **Plan 3-5 weekends to stop and take time for these adventures.**

This Woman's Work (This Month)

- ★ **Go on the first adventure by yourself.**
- ★ **Invite a friend, family member, or child for the others...** *if you decide to open that time to others.*

March

" I Will Create A Place of Peace in My Life "

We all deserve a bit of peace in our lives. Your place of peace may be on your living room couch, or you may find it while preparing dinner in the kitchen. Your serenity may lie within another human being, or you may find peace in spending time with a child, your significant other, or a grandparent.

No matter where it is, how you find it, or who you share it with, it is important to find your peace. After a long, busy day, your place of peace is where you want to go to relax. Your peace can be drinking wine while watching mindless television. It can be reading passages in the bible. It is up to you to find your place of peace. Your place of peace will be important when it seems like life is not slowing down, or things in your personal life are in disarray.

Find your place of peace and claim it. Make a goal to spend at least an hour a day in your space of peace. You will not regret it.

— Arielle Griffin

This Woman's Work (Today)

- ★ List out 10 ways in which you can find peace in your day-to-day life.
- ★ Brainstorm ways to incorporate these things into your regular pattern.
- ★ Take the time to schedule opportunities for peace daily, weekly, monthly, *and annually*.

I Am Proud to Be A Woman

Genesis is the book of beginnings. There, we find the creation story. God spoke; the heavens and the earth became. When it came to humanity, both man and woman were fashioned by God's hand—given God's personal touch, His breath—with woman being formed with the rib taken from man.

And it was very good.

For man, God created a helpmeet. the adjective *meet*—meaning suitable, comparable, or corresponding—stresses that woman, unlike the animals, can be truly one with man.[2] That means woman can enjoy full fellowship and partnership in humanity's God-given task of rule and dominion.[3] *So... no, ma'am! There will be no submission to inferiority here!*

Woman... with her inexplicable, incomparable beauty and mystique... there is just something about how she radiates her way of being while she works and as she loves and lives. Woman gives birth to future generations being full of creativity, innovation, nurture, and motherly love even with a barren womb. You... are woman, perfectly suitable, equal, and fully capable.

She is woman!

I am proud that I am her, and she is me.

— Dr. Latisha D. Reeves Henry

Say Aloud: **I Am Proud to Be A Woman!**

---

[2] Gen 2:20; Gen 2:24
[3] Gen 1:27–28

April

"My Body is My Temple"

Your body is your temple, they say. Well...

...my body has stretch marks, extra skin, scars from surgeries, extra fat where I don't want it and THIGHS that are best friends because they have been so close and touching for as long as I can remember!!!!!!! However, my body IS my temple.

See, it doesn't matter so much the look of the outer temple as it matters the look of the inner. It is the inner temple that carries us through tragedy, which is why we are still here, still loving, and still leading—sometimes without even knowing. It is necessary to always remember that we, as women, carry the universe. Your soul and how you love is what will be remembered; these are what will continue even after you're gone. the way you impacted people's lives will carry on. You are only a vessel to carry out God's love and will. You are so important to God that He gave you the responsibility of nurturing his people.

God loves women so much that He gave us the ability to love, to birth life, to nurture... *and to lead men in a way that makes them think their ideas are always their own.* Who runs the world, you say? Well, I believe you already know the answer. Now, claim your place at the table, and love yourself as God does, with all the outer flaws. Love the being He created, but also know that it is not good for you to continue self-defeating behavior—God did not create you for that.

Love the outer you as much as the inner you love His people without effort. Be who God called you to be. Be the vessel and honor your temple.

— Stephanie Hamilton Muwunganirwa

"

I Am Imperfect.
I Am Flawed.
And That's Perfectly Okay!

"

Imperfections are what make us human! Though there should not be a need to forgive yourself for your imperfections—not in your physical appearances, but in your behaviors or what you may see as flaws. Extend *yourself* the same grace and willingness to forgive as you extend to others. Use the same reassuring, encouraging, "You got this!" voice on yourself as you would with anyone else.

We are human, with daily occurrences that will either have us aligned with our goals and dreams or potentially take us off course. the goal is to get back on track, get back up, and keep moving forward. Leveling up takes time, patience, grace, and most importantly... forgiveness.

If need be, check yourself! Review your past decisions, specifically those you aren't proud of. Take a moment to reflect on what you did, who you did it with, and how it made you feel. What sparked joy? What was draining? What stretched you and made you stronger? Now, take all the time you need to create and design a life that you truly want, one which you can be proud of. Consider what needs shifting in your life.

Self-reflection is indeed humbling, but it's inspiring as well because it's all about what YOU can do for YOU. Love yourself through the process, imperfections, flaws, and all.

— Monique Carter

Say Aloud: **I'm Imperfect and Flawed *and That is Okay!***

April

I Am Not Ashamed

Why should I be ashamed?

Life is all about making mistakes.

What do I have to be ashamed of?

There is nothing new under the sun.

The same mistakes that I am making in life have already been made a million times over.

I should only be ashamed of my mistakes if I am not learning anything from the lessons. That's not me, of course, because I am fearfully and wonderfully made, even in the midst of my mistakes. So, what do I personally have to be ashamed of?

If someone asked you what you are most ashamed of, you might mention something from your past, but why should you because ashamed of something in your past when your past experiences have made you who you are today.

Everything I have experienced in the past has made me into the young woman I am today. There is no mistake that we can make that will totally take us out... unless we allow it to, so don't be ashamed of the things of your past any longer. Allow that weakness to become your strength in God. Use that story to show others how God has worked in your life to bring you out of your old and into your new.

— Kenajawa LaShawn

Say Aloud: **I Am Not Ashamed**

April

I Will Be Confident

Confidence is great. Arrogance is not. on your life's journey, be sure to remain humble and continue to seek both God and knowledge. Confidence is contagious, and it can spread like wildfire when it is properly lit. Confidence is needed to remain motivated to accomplish your goals.

Regardless of what others may think or say—if you firmly believe in what you're doing—don't allow others to persuade you against it. People are not only critical of themselves, but people are critical of others, too. So, no matter how perfect or imperfect you are, someone will always have something to critique or judge you upon. Let them talk! You just continue posting without that filter and stay true to yourself!!

— Erika Harp

April

Confidence is Established Through Preparation!

Preparation and practice are vital in order to establish and increase your confidence level. Do you remember your first public speaking event? If you prepared, you probably practiced for days or weeks in front of your parents, your parent's friends, your friends, your extended family, or whoever else would listen! Did you feel prepared after all that practice? You should have.

During preparation and practice, you have the opportunity to play out different scenarios. Imagine not being prepared or not having practiced. How confident do you think you would be speaking on the topic? Probably not so much. So...

When it comes to being confident... BE PREPARED, and you'll do just fine!

Remember, confidence is established through preparation!

— Erika Harp

April

I Am A Lady of Purpose

Oxford Dictionary defines purpose as the reason for which something is done, created, or exists. We were each created with great purpose in mind. Everything is working together for our good, according to Romans 8:28[4]. That means that the good, the bad, and even the ugliest of circumstances are divinely connected to our purpose.

God alone knows the plans He has for each of us and assures us that it is to prosper and not harm us, to bring us to an expected end.[5] When God uniquely created us, destiny was on His mind. the journey He orchestrated has led us to be poised, postured, and positioned to impact the world in such a way that change has no choice but to come when we take our rightful place.

Queen Hadassah—or Esther, as she is most often called—had to pause and rethink the narrative when fear took a seat on her shoulder. Indeed, she rose to the occasion when her

---

[4] KJV
[5] Jeremiah 29:11

cousin Mordecai reminded her that her ascension to the throne had occurred for her to play a part in saving the Jews.

You and I are also here for divine impact. We have been given authority for such a time as this. You are a lady of purpose born of purpose, reared on purpose, who has overcome for purpose. Let that move you to action. Let Jesus drive you, and purpose guide you, to leave the world better than you found it. Let earth proclaim that its inhabitants are better because you lived... on purpose!

— Dr. Latisha D. Reeves Henry

April

God is on My Side, and. . . I Am Enough

It took me a long time to believe I was enough.
It took me a long time to realize that it doesn't matter who thinks I am enough.
It took me a long time to believe that God thinks I am enough.
That's all that matters.
No one else has to agree. No one else has to tell me.
As long as God and I know I am enough, that's all I need.
The reality is, I will always come up short in human eyes. It doesn't matter.
All that should resonate with me is how God sees me.
God is my creator, and He knows all I'm capable of.
There's no way I should ever doubt who He has called me to be.
No matter who doesn't like it. No matter who doesn't see it.
No matter who agrees.
No matter who leaves.
God is on my side, and that's all I care about.

— Coach Latoya Kight

April

I Am Fearfully and Wonderfully Made

We are required to look the part, play the role, stand in the gap, know the answers, fix the problems, and do it well... in *stilettos*... all before 8:00 am... DAILY! There are deadlines to meet and people to see. to say that life can be a bit overwhelming is quite an understatement. One of the side effects of living in perpetual busy-ness is losing our true sense of personal identity and worth. We become human doings instead of beings.

Each of us is fearfully and wonderfully made, created with a purpose, and divinely designed. Every detail—from hips to lips and fingertips—makes up your "uniquely you" amazing self. You are completely original with a sphere of influence that is made for you alone.

Take some time today to reflect on the richness of your gifts, the magnificent complexities of YOUR purpose, and the beauty of your imperfections. Today, make it *necessary* to embrace your way of being impactful in the places where you find yourself. Today, tell yourself, "I am fearfully and wonderfully made," and then... *believe it!*

— Dr. Latisha D. Reeves Henry

This Woman's Work (Today)

- ★ *Today, read Psalm 139:14.*
- ★ *Write out the verse in your own words.*
- ★ *Read Proverbs 31.*
- ★ *Take time to jot down your thoughts.*
- ★ *Write down how these Bible entries affirm you.*

10

April

"

I am a Virtuous Woman! That's ME!

"

I am a virtuous woman! That's me! I stick to my standards, no matter what! I don't let the opinions of people who don't live with morals or values change my views.

My virtue is important. It made me who I am. It shifts me from being broken to being confident, and it adds a stride to my walk that can't be messed with. It adds value to me that can't be shaken. I love who I have become because of my refusal to lower my standards. It's vital that I hold on to the very things that formed me into the person I worked so hard to be. I can't allow brief gratification to get in the way of being virtuous.

My legacy depends on my virtue.

My children need it.

God requires it.

— Coach Latoya Kight

11

April

"

I Matter

"

Psalm 139 reminds us that we are fearfully and wonderfully made with God having total, complete knowledge of who we are but caring for us anyway. Philippians Chapter 2 makes us aware that it is God who created us and wills us to work and to do according to His good pleasure so that there is no need for us to compare ourselves, our works, our businesses, our callings, our families, our bodies, or anything else to another.

We are so cared for, so intricately and uniquely designed, with purposed assignments attached only to us specifically and individually as God designated.

There will be struggles, toxic relationships, and people who take us for granted. Failures and life's vicissitudes can lead us to believe that we don't matter, yet let me point you to your Creator, the Lover of your very soul, who has it written that you do matter.

John 10:28 and Isaiah 49:16 says that those who are willing to receive such truth have let on God an indelible mark never to be removed.

I DO MATTER.
YOU DO MATTER.

There is no thing, and no one, who can ever change that, so go make your way in the world like you know that you are absolutely necessary... because you are.

— Dr. Latisha D. Reeves Henry

April

"

I Am Worthy

"

One of the most beautiful experiences is to be chosen. As a young girl with very little athletic ability, I was seldom chosen to be on anyone's team, whether basketball, kickball, racing, or flag football. No kid welcomes these moments. Neither do adults.

Many times, we have rehearsed the negatives of not being chosen as frequently as a favorite morning meditation—over and over. the failure, bad choices, abuse, misuse, and betrayals perpetuate against us.

Maybe it is harsh words spoken over you and to you that cause you to feel unworthy. It is time to put a stop to the constant replay. Let Romans chapter 8 bring the comfort of transforming truth. You are chosen—equipped for positive impact. You are loved by the Creator for no other reason than because it is what the Creator has chosen to do. the element of performing to earn is overthrown. the need for perfection for acceptance is reversed. You are worthy because you are a prized treasure. Worthy since the day you were born, no matter the circumstances surrounding your birth or the issues permeating your life. You are worthy of love. You are worthy of peace. You are worthy of another chance. You are worthy of forgiveness. You are worthy of God's best. Declare it to be because IT IS SO.

You Are Worthy!

— Dr. Latisha D. Reeves Henry

April

" I Will Nurture My Inner Woman "

Some days are easier than others. Some days have amazing highs. Others have interesting lows. Women are emotional beings. We carry the weight of the world on our shoulders, in our eyes, and deep down in our souls. We are strong but fragile. We are bold yet meek. We are amazing in our own unique ways. Even with all the amazing qualities we share, women still hurt in silence, together. We still bleed on the inside and smile on the outside.

That has to change. We must take back our best attributes and really be our best selves from the inside out. We have to be the types of women that we want our daughters to admire. We don't want them to bear the unnecessary burdens we' ourselves have already learned to carry so well.

Let's take the time to nurture our inner woman because if we give up on *her*, then what do we really have?

— Chantell Williams

I Will Encounter and Defeat My Ego

Our ego will always be something we have to encounter and defeat. As soon as we overcome being jealous or doubting ourselves in one area of our lives, another situation arises where it seems as if someone else is taking our spotlight. Your ego yells, "When is it my turn?"

First, know that there is more than enough room for spotlights to shine on each of us. the universe has no limitations. Second, sometimes the universe is shining brighter in another area in order to direct your attention elsewhere. in these moments, the darkness can represent areas you have neglected or tasks and responsibilities on which you have procrastinated.

The next time your ego arises in the midst of someone else being in the spotlight, take a moment and look at your shadows and see what progress your ego is trying to direct your attention to.

— Kwanza Yates

I Am Tuned in to My Intuition

Ladies, we have been blessed with a heightened sense of intuition. Intuition is defined as instinctive knowledge that is not obtained by reason or perception.[6] This intuition is God speaking to you and *through* you. This

---

[6] Webster's Dictionary

blessed enhanced sense is not only to be used to tell you when your man is cheating *(as some may think)*, but it also informs you when to take a different route to work. Intuition tells you when to talk to a stranger, and more importantly… when NOT to talk to a stranger. It whispers, "You need to take a mental break," and it yells, "He is NOT the one!" Intuition discerns the difference between a child's minor tummy ache and something more serious.

Ladies, we have been blessed by God with an awesome connection to Him that can transform us into Wonder Women every day, but only if we tune in.

What is your intuition telling you today? Are you tuned in?

— Kwanza Yates

16 April

I Will Silence My Inner Critic

I have an inner critic, and I gave her a name. Her name is Petty Penelope. I named her Petty Penelope because the inner voice in my head is SOOOOO petty. Oftentimes, the voice in my head goes totally against what's in my heart.

You know that feeling when you know you have done the best that you can, and that voice in your head STILL finds everything you've done wrong... that's your inner critic speaking to you. That voice that is in your head when everyone in the room is saying you've done a great job, but that voice finds something to say that cancels out everything great that was said... Yup! Inner Critic! *(Petty Penelope for me.)*

What others say to you is great, but what matters most is what you say to yourself. Silence your inner critic by managing your self-talk. *Are you talking kindly to everyone else while being unkind to yourself?* It's time to start practicing being nice to yourself. Silencing your inner critic will help you to feel better about success and help you to celebrate your small wins. You are worthy of every accomplishment you have achieved. You are worthy of all the honor because of all the tremendous gains you have made this year! Silence your inner critic with positive, kind words to yourself. Use affirmations and manage your self-talk so that the next time your inner critic says you can't, tell your Petty Penelope that you can, and you will!

— Coach Mechelle Canady

April 17

I Am a Woman of Integrity

Being a woman of integrity is a valuable trait. It means you can be trusted. It means you value honesty. It will help you become honorable in the eyes of those you come in contact.

Integrity is something you should always hold onto. Aim daily to be a woman of integrity.

As for me, I refuse to be anything else, especially not for notoriety or to be in a relationship. I will stay true to who I am to gain the acceptance of God only. God's view of me is the only thing that matters. When I value the view of others more than His, I dishonor Him. I never want to intentionally do anything that would cause God to frown upon me. I want my children to look at their mom as an example of integrity. I want my husband to trust that I will always operate in integrity. I want those watching me to see a woman who daily strives to be full of integrity.

No matter the place or circumstance, if I stay true to the real me, then God can bless me abundantly.

— Coach Latoya Kight

Say Aloud: **I Am a Woman of Integrity**

I Will Value My Health

Health is defined as a state of COMPLETE well-being that is free from disease and infirmity. Living a healthy life possess a challenge for many, yet I want to challenge you to reset your life. Take a vow to live a healthy life that is complete and whole.

Your health is impacted by what you eat, think, hear, see, and your response to life experiences. Make a decision to live a life that expresses value in your health. Take small steps in great stride each day. Set aside time to journal. *(This is for your mental health.)* Instead of driving for lunch, take a walk around your office for about 15 minutes and track your steps. Instead of returning a list of phone calls on your break, spend quiet time in your car. Value your personal time—and your health—enough to slow down and prepare a meal for yourself that is filled with lots of colors. the more color, the more diversity of nutrients in your meal. When you value who you are through prioritizing your health, you live life differently.

★ *How have you acknowledged the value of your health?*

— Regina N Roberts

I Will Know My History

Technology has proven to be invaluable. At any given point in this age, we have access to innumerable amounts of information. Social media is flooded with it. the internet never runs out of it. That being true, I can... I MUST... know my history!

I remember hearing the little-known black history facts every morning on the radio. It made me hungry to know more and search for myself. A necessary surgical procedure made me realize how important it was for me to know the history of my family. Seminary and a love for Bible study gave me the desire to discover biblical history. A stolen identity made it imperative to know the history of the country I live in. Whether the focus is cultural, medical, or otherwise, I have decided that now, more than ever, I WILL know my history. Knowing where I have been helps me to know where I am going. It consequently informs why I long to be there.

Google, Siri, and Alexa make a plethora of information, facts, figures, and pictures available in seconds. Doctor's appointments and talks with grand-parents and grand-aunts can be great motivators. I decided that I will know my history because somebody has to stand up and tell the truth about who I am, where I am from, and how I got here. Someone tomorrow needs to know how incredible they are because today we are scholars, kings, queens, doctors, lawyers, orators, historians, preachers, storytellers, bridge-builders, activists, scientists, entrepreneurs, etc. They need to know we struggled, faltered, and failed at some things so that they don't repeat and re-live the same mistakes. Yes, I will know my history so I can talk, laugh, pray, relish in it, and sing—loudly, proudly—'bout how I got over.

— Dr. Latisha D. Reeves Henry

April

My Future is Bright!

As long as there is breath in my body, the future is bright and limitless. I possess so much potential. I just have to tap into it and do the work!

We all may want to achieve our dreams, but it first takes hard work, dedication, and perseverance. Many want the glory, but how many of these are willing to do hard work, the work no one else wants to do? Now, of those, how many would still be so willing to keep going after downfall, after setback, after failure? A lot fewer, and that's why those who persevere, achieve. They know hard work will pay off. They know their potential, so they push forward.

Today, I encourage you to push forward in life. No matter how many times you get knocked down, keep moving forward, knowing the future is bright.

— Brittany Whigham

April

Winning Is Not an Option.
It's the Solution

For a long time, I thought that I would always be plagued with poverty. It's all that I knew. There are not many people in my family who are financially free. Some of you can probably relate to this too.

Because I did not grow up with much guidance on what I needed to do for my future, I found myself just copying what I thought others were doing. for example, I had this false perception that college was all I needed to have a good life, so I got to college and thought that was the end—that's not true!

After a couple of falls in life, I understood that winning was not just an option I had but winning was my solution! I also had to adjust my definition of winning. It is not materialistic or monetary for me. Winning for me means gaining peace and holding on to it. Winning is realizing I have the One who holds all power fighting alongside me. Winning is overcoming my mental battles every day. Winning is breaking generational curses that will set my future family and me free. Winning is realizing I have everything I already need on the inside of me. Therefore, winning is not my option. It is my solution!

— Kenajawa LaShawn

April

"

I Will NOT Fear ME

"

I won't fear who I am created to be any longer.
I will embrace my God-given purpose.
I will be confident in the way God made me.
I won't try to change the things that line up with who God called me
    to be.
I will simply be grateful for who He says I am.
If He saw fit to create me...
    If He is gracious enough to keep me...
There must be something bigger for me.
    There must be something better for me.
There must be something greater for me to do.
I *must* have something important to do,
    so I will walk in all that I am with my head held high.
I will believe in myself.
I won't give up on who God sees me as.
There is no limit to what I can do.
    There's nothing unreachable...
                    ...and...

God can do exceedingly and abundantly above
all I can ask or think.

— Coach Latoya Kight

I Will Nurture the Lady in Me

As a little girl, your mother taught you to sit up straight because that's good posture. She taught you to speak when spoken to because that shows respect. She said, "Ladies are to be seen and not heard," which shows poise. She told you to always say, "Please," "May I," and "Thank you," because that is good manner. She taught you to always forgive because that shows grace. She taught you that crying is not a sign of weakness but a moment of strength.

These are just a few of a lady's skills, yet there is so much more that shows who we are as women. See, we have been shaped and molded to be nothing less than a lady. Let's take a moment and thank the women in our lives who took the time to correct us and call us to accountability. the constant nurturing and love that was and is still being poured into us daily is what made us who we are today.

To all the ladies in the world,
we salute you!

— Chantell Williams

Affirmation Journal

- ★ What does it mean to nurture the lady in me?
- ★ How can I better nurture the lady in me?
- ★ What haven't I considered?
- ★ How can I encourage others to support me in these efforts?

Say Aloud: I Will Nurture the Lady in Me

I Will Get to Know God.
I Will Get to Know Myself.

Everyone makes it seem like being single is such a dread. If you are not in a known relationship, you're the outcast. This was the hardest battle for me after finding my relationship with God. Initially, my relationship with Him wasn't enough. Being alone was just a scary thought. I felt pressured by all I saw on social media, so it left me making unwarranted decisions in my relationship with God. Until...

Until I realized that my time of singleness is actually a special time. God helped me to realize that this time of singleness, is nothing about being alone at all. During this time, women are meant to spend quality time with God and develop our relationship with him. It's time to figure ourselves out and figure out what we like.

I wasted a lot of time in relationships hoping that others would love me when I didn't even know how to love myself.

Instead of spending your single season seeking your next relationship, spend this time:

   ★   Learning to love God
   ★   Learning to love yourself
   ★   Getting a head start on your bucket list
   ★   Buying yourself all the things you like
   ★   Building some meaningful friendships
   ★   Taking yourself out

You'll be glad you did!

— Kenajawa LaShawn

April

I Am the BEST Brand of DIVA There IS!

You call me a diva? Well, let me be the best diva that I can be! There's NO comparison. I'm in a league of my own. I'm sassy. I'm smart. I'm sexy. I'm a BOSS!

I'm an original. You will never find another like me. I will walk with my head held high. I will talk with a force that no man can deny. I will demand attention when I walk into the room.

I'm fierce! There's nothing holding me back. There's nothing that anyone can do or say to me to make me believe that I'm not everything that I am. I will let the world know who I am, and I won't waiver. I will not hide in the background. I was born to SHINE, and I will shine my light SO bright.

I am bold! I am courageous! I'm a force to be reckoned with!

— Coach Latoya Kight

April

I AM A GEM!

Sitting on the side of the bed in tears! I'm not where I ought to be, but—Thank God—I'm not where I use to be.

As little women, we have our lives all planned out: what we will be, where we will live, who we will marry, and how many children we will have by the time we are 30. Age 30 is on the way or has arrived for some of us, and we are not prepared. There are things we felt we have worked to get that just haven't happened for us. There are also things we've avoided to make sure we stayed on track, but somewhere along the lines, we took a wrong turn.

Today, I encourage you to get back on track! Yes, you are beautiful! Yes, you have a big amazing personality! Yes, you are loyal! You are a great mother, sister, cousin, niece, and aunt! Sometimes, it may feel like all of this is not enough, but I assure you that *it is*! the greatest gift God can give you is your destiny, so shine sister, SHINE! You Are A GEM!

— Chantell Williams

April

"

Always Look for the Rainbow

"

My windows to the world! Wow!

I LOVE my eyes and all that they've revealed to me over my lifetime.

When thinking of the journey our eyes have taken us on, where do we start, and what do we remember? Good stuff? Exciting stuff? Sad stuff? Exceptional stuff? Unbelievable stuff? Scary stuff?

I see the love of my life and the amazing children God blessed us with. I think of their journeys into adulthood and... WOW! I have five grandbabies. in life, I saw pain, fear, wonderment, confusion... Then, we all experienced great joy when they—the grands—came into our lives. I tear up just thinking about it! And yes... While I've seen the bad, ugly devastation of heartache and what weather can bring, I always looked for the rainbow!

★ Where and what are the good, bad, and ugly things your eyes have witnessed?

★ How did your life change in those instances?

★ Where do you still need to experience and see hope, healing, love, and wholeness in your life?

Look to Jesus, the Pioneer and Perfecter of your faith. Let Him in. Then cast ANY burdens you may have on Him. It doesn't matter how long you've been holding onto the pain. Give it ALLLLLL up! Share praise with Him and someone who may need to hear what you've witnessed and recovered from. You are unique and wonderfully made, and you are made in God's image! in His eyes, you are as beautiful as a rainbow.

— MommyV

April 28

I Am Always Doing Me

Let's be truthful: you may never set foot in Paris, never fly on a private jet, never swim off the Amalfi Coast, never purchase a Bugatti, and never sip champagne in the penthouse suite. And does it really matter if these were never YOUR goals to begin with? You couldn't even spell Bugatti before it showed up in a popular song. Don't seek things you were never meant to find in the first place. When you go after another woman's goals, you end up stressed, unsatisfied, and unsuccessful, and you won't even know why. It's because you are following someone down their path of life rather than carving out your own.

When you begin to walk in YOUR destiny, which can only be obtained from within, then you will realize it's not about trying to become the next "so and so," but about being the one and only YOU! And when you realize just how FIERCE you are, if you never get to do those things mentioned above, you will still always be happy and satisfied because you will always be doing you!

— Kwanza Yates

April

" I Will Be A Better ME! "

Always improving.

That is my daily motto. It is what I strive for—to always be working to be a better me.

Each day is filled with multiple opportunities to try to be better, do better, and just live better. I try to focus more on me in situations, and I consider how any situation can be a learning opportunity for my own personal growth.

Every day is filled with personal development opportunities. You just have to see them for what they are. Traffic, however annoying it may be, can be a learning opportunity. Traffic requires patience and perseverance. How many times have you prayed for patience? Boom! Traffic can teach you to slow down. Learn to ask questions, but instead of asking, "Why is this happening to me?" ask, "What is this teaching me?" and you'll be sure to experience growth as a person. Asking the right questions of life will help you with personal development. Those questions will help you be a better you.

— Brittany Whigham

Affirmation Journal

★ What trends am I noticing about myself?
★ What needs to be adjusted?
★ In what ways can I be a better me?
★ What value will be gained in the end?

Say Aloud: I Will Be A Better ME!

I Accept Myself as I Am

Comparison is a killer.

In our current society, it has become almost instinctive to compare ourselves to others. We are comparing ourselves to the newest celebrity or even comparing ourselves to the co-worker with the new car. Don't get me wrong; this has been a struggle of mine as well. the constant comparison eventually causes us to devalue ourselves. We become... just not good enough...

Say Aloud:

> We make the mistake **I accept myself as I am. I am good enough to be loved. I am good enough to be accepted. I am good enough to see myself as valuable.**

We make the mistake of rating our own value against things that are only momentary. Instagram will not be forever. Twitter, Snapchat, likes, comments, and shares don't last forever, either!

Once I began to establish my values in God, I was able to accept myself for who God made me be. So even the things the world says that are not right about me, I am now fine accepting because I know who establishes my value, and it's not this WORLD!

— Kenajawa LaShawn

Say Aloud: I Accept Myself as I Am!

Self Help!

May 1

Change Requires Commitment.

Change requires commitment, and commitment is a choice. Change is not for the weak or uncommitted—it will challenge you. *Commit to it!* Stay committed so you can remain motivated to BE the change you want to see.

I once read, "Motivation doesn't last, neither do baths... That's why they are recommended daily."

Daily motivation is what will keep you committed to the change. Books, sermons, inspirational messages, affirmations, vision boards, etc., are all ways to assist in sustaining commitment. Stay committed, and you can stay motivated until the end!

— Erika Harp

May 2

I Will Use My 1,440

Do you ever feel like there isn't enough time in the day? We are all consumed with working, commuting, cooking, cleaning, spending time with family, and the list of responsibilities goes on and on and on! What if I told you that you have 1,440 opportunities every single day to begin the things you set in your mind to accomplish?

There are 1,440 minutes in a day, and every minute that passes is a minute you could be using to begin or finish YOUR goals and desires.

How much of your 1,440 minutes are you allotting for your goals and desires? Not much?

Today, commit to doing more.

Use your 1,440.

— Erika Harp

May

I Will Follow My Passion

There is no blueprint already written to accomplish what YOU have a passion for. It's what YOU have a passion for! **When God gives you a burning passion for something, passion is what leads the path to creating it and seeing it through.** There is no GPS with right or left directions to accomplish what YOU have passion for. However, while we may not have that, we do have something that is a great help… and it's at your fingertips. GOOGLE! *(I call the Internet… GOOGLE)!!!!* by using an invaluable resource like the internet, you can create and develop goals—strategies, business plans, marketing campaigns, and more—so the passion you commit to following has a path that you must follow to see it through to the end.

Commit to your passion—not to the path you take to accomplish it. Why? Because you may get off the path to accomplishing it, but it's all part of the journey.

— Erika Harp

Say Aloud: **I Will Follow My Passion**

"

I Am Willing. . .

"

I Am Willing...

With my heart pounding and my mind full of thoughts
of the unknown,
I am willing to push forward with faith in the Almighty.
I am willing because my trust is in my own strength
and ability to fly,
not in the strength of the branch upon which I stand.
I am willing to go after that dream,
that goal, and all my desires.
I am willing to love unconditionally—yet wisely.
I am willing to take a chance,
with the possibility of failure.
Failure is a lesson learned,
so I am willing to take another step to get it right. I am
willing to allow my God to lead while I walk in my calling.
I am willing to stand alone.
I am willing to go it on my own.
I am willing to be courageous and take that risk
even if it means an outcome completely different
from what I envisioned.
I am willing to do it, and do it NOW,
as time waits for no one.
I am willing to be vulnerable, raw, and open—
for this is where I can have the most impact.
For my purpose, and to fulfill my calling,
I am willing to do all these things.
For myself, for me, I am Willing...

— Monique Carter

May

I Will Not Be Complacent!

Yell it with me!!!!

I will not get complacent!

One of God's most precious moments is giving us what He wants us to have and the things that we wish for! Yes, folks! God is the God of things wished for! Look it up! It's in the Bible. That being said, God doesn't want us to ever just be satisfied with just enough. He doesn't want us to struggle, and He sure doesn't want us to just stay where we are spiritually, mentally or financially. God wants us to live well!!! Yes, we should be thankful for all He has already given us, but God wants more for our lives.

In your life, don't be ashamed to ask God, "What's next?" He expects us to expect more. He expects us to ask for it, and God expects us to **believe** for what we ask. Trust me... When you ask God for what you will, you are not being selfish or greedy when you are asking and moving in His will. Let that be your self-check when you have the desire to want more. Follow this especially when you're not asking him for more. Be wise, stay humble, but don't get complacent in your expectations!

— Cortney D. Surrency, AC-CHC

Say Aloud: **I Will Follow My Passion**

6 May

The Sky Is the Limit!

"I have an idea!"

That's how growth happens.

Something inside you is crying out to be born. What an exciting time for you! You are about to embark on something new, so listen to your instincts, and... GO for IT!

Plan! Write it down. Try, try, and try again! Don't give up. You are learning with each step you take.

Understand that your passion is yours to develop and present, so... ask for help! Do not be afraid.

What are your passions? Cooking? Writing? Politics? Owning your own business? Teaching? Yes, the sky's the limit.

— MommyV

---

7 May

If You Want Something, Go Get It

Initially, when I began my college career, I was a computer science major. I quickly realized this was not the right fit for me and decided to change my major. Through some careful consideration and a look at career opportunities, I decided to switch my studies to social work. I knew that if I wanted to major in social work, I would need to obtain my BSW, MSW, and eventually LCSW. During my freshman year of college, I began to explore MSW programs. I decided where I wanted to attend school for my MSW and made this my goal.

By the end of my BSW program, I had completed two internships, worked two jobs, and completed a work-study job through my institution. This was not a simple task by any means; however, I knew what my goals were and that I needed to achieve them.

The day I received my acceptance to my dream graduate school program, I was so excited. This was the first time I had cried tears of happiness. All my work had paid off. I completed my master's degree in one year by admittance into the accelerated program and landed my dream internship at the end. This led to my current career as a medical social worker. I am currently working towards my LCSW, which will take a few years.

If you want something, go get it! Only through determination and perseverance will your dreams be made possible.

Networking is key.

A positive attitude is key.

Success is key.

— Arielle Griffin

Affirmation Journal
- ★ In what ways can I take advantage of networking?
- ★ In what ways can I take advantage of positivity?
- ★ In what ways can I take advantage of success?
- ★ How can I use these together to go after what I want in life?

May

If the Door Doesn't Open, I Will Keep on KNOCKING!

I'm sure we all have heard the saying,

"Write the vision and make it plain."

We all have goals, dreams, and ambitions for life.

I'm sure the road to your specific dreams was not laid out for you like you wanted or was even remotely close to what you had in mind. When you faced this, you either kept on pushing until the dream became a reality or you kept the vision in mind until you were given the right tools to take the first step.

No matter what your process has been, make sure you never take no for an answer! Consider "No," only as a "Next!" Step in front of your next door and knock. Kick if you must, but never—and I mean never—quit. Nothing of great value or substance was done in a day, and your success will be no different.

Remember, Queen, be bold, and take life on.

Don't let life take you on.

— Chantell Williams

This Woman's Work [Today]

★ List 3 areas in your life where you are being denied.
★ List some steps you can take to resist these *Nos*?
★ List 3 additional areas of opportunity where you will work while you keep knocking on the other doors.

May

Life Can Be So Overwhelming, But I Keep Pushing

The trials and tribulations of life try to weigh me down.

The blows that life throws try to hinder me.

The hard situations that I face try to knock me out.

I can't let life win.

I can't let the enemy overpower me.

I can't go down without a fight.

I must push through.

I must press my way.

I can't let what I see overshadow what I believe.

I'm stronger than that. I'm better than that.

I'm greater than that.

God is on my side.

He is the great ruler,

so I know I can overcome anything.

— Coach Latoya Kight

Affirmation Journal

★ In what areas am I currently overwhelmed?

★ What do I do to push through in these areas?

★ What additional tools can I use to help me?

"

Every New Day Brings Me Closer to My Dreams

"

Perception shapes our actions, reactions, and our motivations; It can also stifle our productivity. If we get distracted by our own busy-ness, we forget that the daily grind brings us closer to our success once our energy is channeled in the direction of our dreams. We are often the greatest detractor from achieving our dreams. When we believe that we are too old, broke, skinny, fat, uncreative, busy—or any of the other things we tell ourselves—we slowly begin to sabotage our dreams because we are afraid.

We must NOT allow fear to win. It is time to change the narrative. Rather than despise, ignore or live in frustration because we haven't yet reached the goal, let's look forward to every day as another opportunity to work the vision we have written. Pull out that journal, that notepad, that laptop, and cross one more task off the to-do list today. Take the steps that lead you to your dream. Do what you can, while you can, each day, until you find that your work is done.

Proverbs 6:6 KJV says, "Consider the ways of the ant and be wise." Every day, your ordered steps bring you closer to your dream. Success has not eluded you. You are right on schedule. Your detours are not denials, so come on... take another step. Set your gaze as sharp as a laser and aim it at your dream. You are closer today than yesterday, and tomorrow, you will be closer than you are today. Plan the work and work your plan until you see what you have said. Lean into your vision and move forward!

— Dr. Latisha D. Reeves Henry

Mistakes Do Not Equal Failure.
They Are an Experience to Learn From

If someone asked you today, "What's the biggest mistake that you have made?" what would you say? If it makes it easier, write your answer somewhere in the margin of this page. Next, ask yourself, "What do you remember learning from that?" Our mistakes do not equal failure; rather, they provide us with the lessons that we gain from experience.

Don't allow mistakes to control your life. the Bible promises me that God doesn't even keep a record of my wrongs, so why should I? Take those moments that you consider mistakes and turn them into a list of lessons learned.

— Kenajawa LaShawn

12

May

I Will Be A Better Student

It can be so easy to fall behind in school. This statement applies to any level of school but proves particularly true for college. There is no one there to make sure you are completing assignments or studying for tests.

You are accountable for yourself, yet other students can also be instrumental to your success. If you are spending time with people who are not completing assignments on time or who neglect school to have fun, your circle needs to change. the people you choose to spend your time with or have in your circle can make all the difference. Most times, if you are around those who strive for success, you will tend to do the same.

Do not be satisfied with sub-par or average performance, and always aim to do better. School does not always come easy for everyone. Success for you may mean spending extra hours in the library or skipping that campus event that looks like fun. Aim for the top. If you aren't doing this already, be a better student, it will pay off in the long run.

— Arielle Griffin

May

I Own My Choices.
I Own My Changes.

We constantly have to make choices. Sometimes, these choices can lead to BIG changes. A new career path. Move to a new state. Go back to school. Changes such as these can seem drastic to the outside world. But you know what? Sometimes a drastic change is exactly what's needed to thrust you forward. to throw you smack dab into the middle of your destiny.

You can't always baby-step your way through life, and you can't always sit around and wait for everyone else to get on board with your vision. Sometimes, you have to step out and simply do it, and not just do it, but do it like it's never been done before.

Change won't always look the way you want it to, and that's ok. Everyone won't always be on board with your change, and that is ok also, but when you dig deep and move forward with what is best for *you*, you will always be owning your choices, and you will own your changes.

— Kwanza Yates

14 May

I Will Go for What I Want in Life, Even If I Have to Do It Afraid

There are things you are supposed to do. There are things you are supposed to go after. There are things you are supposed to accomplish. You have to go after these things no matter what. You have to go after them even if you are afraid. You have to go after the dream, not knowing what is next. You have to go after your purpose with all the faith and trust in God that you have.

Go after your goals with every little bit of faith you can muster up and every little bit of courage you can gather. the next trial, the next tribulation can throw you off, and it's true: you don't want to lose. You don't want to miss out on your opportunity, but no one has to know that you're afraid. No one has to know you doubt yourself. No one has to know that you second-guess everything. No one has to know that you're weak even at this very moment! Just keep pushing.

Keep going, no matter what. Even though it may seem bleak, and even though you don't always trust what you see, trust in the God that you serve. Do it, even if you're afraid.

— Coach Latoya Kight

Say Aloud: I Will Go for What I Want in Life!

"

I Push Myself to MOVE. . .
Even When I Don't Want to

"

All days are not good days. Let's be honest... some days are rough. It is in those days that you have to keep the faith that there is a reason for your being here. Living your life with intention and positivity is what is necessary to reach your full potential. You see, there are times when you won't want to move. When you are tired and when you are hurting, these moments are the ones when you should do just that—you should move!

Move through so you can get to the other side. Push yourself to move when you don't want to, even if that means pushing yourself to do something you wouldn't normally do.

I personally am not a fan of speaking in front of groups of people, but when I am given the opportunity, I don't allow fear to let me say no. I prepare myself for what I am going to say, and I execute. When the opportunity comes for you to say, "YES!" say it, and allow God to prepare you for your greatness.

He does not set you up to fail.

— Stephanie Hamilton Muwunganirwa

Affirmation Journal

★ Where in life have I slowed down?
★ What have I been avoiding in life?
★ What do I need to do to push myself in these areas?
★ How can I enlist a friend or two to help me?

I Must Pay the Cost to Be the Boss

In life, you must be able to make sacrifices. You have to be willing to take chances. You must be able to leap when you don't even know where you will land. to be the boss, you won't always know what will happen on the other side. That means that you must take risks that you may not have ever taken before.

If you go after what no one else sees, be willing to keep going forward despite any negativity, problems, or obstacles around you. You must continue to go forth and continue to go after your dreams and goals, no matter what comes your way. Why? Because you are a BOSS!

You must make sacrifices.

You will go through trials and tribulations while dealing with attacks that will come against you, your life, your business, and your opportunities. the simple fact that the enemy doesn't want you to be great means that there are things you are going to lose. There are things you are going to have to be without, and relationships and opportunities that will end. People and situations are going to hurt you. Sometimes, these problems are going to make you want to give up. You must keep pushing through because, at the end of it all, it will be worth it.

Pay the price now! Don't quit and live to regret it because, in the end, you will see how it all works out for your good.

— Coach Latoya Kight

Say Aloud: **I Must Pay the Cost to Be the Boss**

May

"

I Better DO IT. . .
and Not Just TALK About Doing It!

"

I'm ALL for speaking goals and desires into existence, ladies, but I need you to *work* for it more than you *talk* about it. We all know faith without works is dead. Well, goals without work are dead too!

I urge you to create goals and write down your strategies to accomplish those goals and fulfill your desires. the strategies that you create are the action steps needed for you to achieve your goals. A goal without a strategy is just a wish, and wishes don't require any work. I can guarantee that if you wish for your goals to be accomplished—they won't be. You can't expect to accomplish goals without work.

Work on your goals.

Don't just talk about 'em.

— Erika Harp

May

"

I Will Practice Good Habits!!!

"

A declaration to practice good habits can evolve into a positive lifestyle change. Many times, I've been asked by others how I developed new habits with such ease and how they could do the same. If I'm honest, developing and practicing good habits isn't easy, but the first step is to JUST DO IT. the next step is to KEEP DOING IT, and the final step is to repeat steps one and two!

Instead of waiting and planning, sometimes the best way to change your eating habits is to choose the *next* meal differently. the best way to read more is to pick up a book and read the intro. the first step to exercise is to start walking.

Every effort of practicing good habits begins with a decision that has many positive actions behind it. Once you make a decision in life and walk it out, the universe comes behind and supports it. Another promising effort in practicing good habits is to establish a partnership with someone who will walk, run, or swim through the journey with you providing feedback, support, and praises where needed.

Write out three habits you want to develop. Then, make a decision and GO!

— Regina N Roberts

19

May

Keep Trying Until Successful, Then Keep Trying Again!

Success is measured by what makes you happy and whole. Success is achieved in the efforts of shooting your best shot, taking any LEAP in life, making lemonade from lemons, and making sweet pies from mud pies. Success is guaranteed when you understand failure, appreciate disappointment, and allow every thread of fear to drive and motivate you to try again.

Success is all about altering your perspective of the life you lead. No matter how many times you fail, sharpen those failures, and try again!

Success is a mindset that you establish achieving Your goals, measured by your expectations accomplished by things you input, and a manifestation of your ownership of what you make it.

Unknown

— Regina N Roberts

If I'm Gonna Stay in My Lane, I Better Slay in My Lane!

YES!

We all know someone who is simply good at anything they set their mind to, but most of us are not built this way. We find that which works for us, and we stick with it, oftentimes mediocrely. We think we have it together because we have a few supporters, and for the most part, we're happy about our little progress. We don't venture out. We stick to old habits and routines, and we completely stop learning and honing our craft.

YES!

If you're going to try something completely outside your norm, then you better spice it up. *Level up!* Study your field, talent, or craft. Pour your heart into it and put your unique spin into your industry. Speak to your clientele and customers and see how you can best serve them. Act as if you had unlimited time, funds, and resources. How much more would you bring it?

YES!

See that vision that just popped in your head... let's make it happen! No need to have half a dozen different goals. Find a solid goal and stick to it! Focus on that and stay in your lane, and if you're gonna stay in your lane, you'd better SLAY in your lane!

— Monique Carter

Say Aloud: **I'm Gonna Stay in My Lane and SLAY!!!**

" I Will Step CONFIDENTLY to the Next Level! "

Wise women know life is a constant teacher because they are lifelong learners. the more they learn, the more they realize that they truly don't know much at all. We're blessed to live in a world that allows us the freedom to educate ourselves *(without limit)*. This journey is meant to be lived and explored, so become immersed in it! Take a journey, especially on the roads less traveled. Become genuinely curious about an area in YOUR life that you either fear, struggle with, or are simply uncomfortable facing. It's less intimidating when you face it head on—it's exciting too!

* Commit to trying something new.
* Commit to meeting new people.
* Commit to having a wider variety of conversations and interactions.
* Learn a different culture by going to a new place.
* *Have a crazy experience!!!*

This is where growth comes from. It happens when we can truly *feel* what increases our vibrations, what scares us, what drives us, and most importantly, what shows you what you don't want! Be courageous! Be bold and step out on faith—get outside of your comfort zone because what if... what if... it actually works for you?! What if you try this new thing, and it becomes the one thing that changes your life forever?! Take that risk on yourself. Begin to invest in you!

— Monique Carter

Say Aloud: **I Will Step Confidently to My Next Level**

I EMBRACE Life. . .
Right Where I Am

I attended a conference some years ago where Lucinda Cross was the guest speaker. One of the things that she said has stuck with me for many years. She said, "You should always strive to be the best, right where you are." That quote has consistently helped me to put things into perspective whenever I lose sight of how valuable my "right now" is.

We get so caught up in trying to get to the next place that we negate where we are at this very moment. Your "right now" has value. You may not be where you want to be, but where you are today has so much to offer you right now. Your today includes things that your tomorrow needs!! You may be suffering life's lessons in your "right now," but take a moment and just think about where you currently are because where you currently are is what is going to get you to where you are eventually going.

Embrace life... right where you are. Take advantage of every opportunity today brings you.

Whenever you use GPS to get to a location, it asks for permission to identify your current location, so... even though you are headed somewhere else... where you are right now is crucial to where you are headed.

— Coach Mechelle Canady

Say Aloud: **I EMBRACE Life. . . Right Where I Am**

Everything in Due Time

The book of Ecclesiastes expresses that to everything there is an appointed time and season in which beautiful things are produced. Understanding the value of time and how it impacts the world and others in your life proves itself at every juncture. Consider your own existence....

Science teaches that the development of a baby takes a nine-month period, and then the baby is birthed. Every stage within a nine-month period is vital to the development of a baby's arrival and to the preparation of a woman's body to withstand the experience of childbirth. Therefore, when a woman's' body tries to resist at any time during the process, the effects can be dangerous to the development of both the mother and child.

Think about your own life. Examine those times when you aborted the seasons in life that needed nurturing, grooming, and sowing. Remember those times you aborted simply waiting until the timing was right. Think about those moments when the time was NOW, and yet you moved too slow or were just too lazy to LEAP or shoot your shot.

In the future, let's choose to no longer make premature decisions based on fear or emotions in the moment that could be detrimental to the health and longevity of a lifelong victory. Let's relish moments of time and allow the essence of time to bring forth that which is beautiful.

Take some time to appreciate the process of growth and preparation. Keep hope alive knowing all will be well because, in DUE time, all things will be beautiful.

— Regina N Roberts

Say Aloud: **Everything in Due Time!**

"

Do Not Rush into Anything

"

There is a time, a space, and a place for everything. Your timeline in this life is not to be compared to anyone else's. Your season for love, passion, relationships, work advancement, and children will happen as they should. God will position you right where you need to be for all your hearts desires to come to fruition, yet there is a task for you as well.

You must be in conversation with him—**Prayer**. This is the first step to aligning yourself with the abundance God has for you. Changing your mindset will help you sustain when the process gets challenging—**Positivity**. Your diligence, hard work, and paying attention to those subtle cues from God will allow you to be confident you are heading in the right direction—**Perseverance**. This life we must live is not meant for you to be in your own bubble with your blinders on. While others are not there as a comparison for the timeline of your life, there is power in fundamental human relationships. Whether they are personal or professional, there is value in getting to know the strengths of other women so you can be leveraged to use your gifts—**Positioning**. Lastly, you must have the tenacity to know what's yours and to claim what's yours—**Persistence**.

— Stephanie Hamilton Muwunganirwa

Say Aloud: Do Not Rush into Anything

I Will Feel the Pain, So I Don't Feel the Regret

When you try to avoid the pain of feelings such as rejection, failure, disappointment, loneliness, loss, and letting go of those things and people that do not serve you, you will always feel the ultimate pain of regret.

You will regret that you didn't take a chance. You will regret that you did not speak your heart. You will regret that you didn't love again. You will regret that you held on when you should've let go, and you will regret that you let go when you should've held on. You will regret you didn't wager your biggest bet on yourself!

On life's journey, pain is inevitable, but the pain of regret is the pain of a missed opportunity. Don't let your fears cause you to feel the ultimate pain of missed opportunities...

...because, *that*...

...you certainly will regret.

— Kwanza Yates

Affirmation Journal

★ What are some situations in life that I am avoiding?
★ What are some conversations that I am avoiding?
★ What are some places that I am avoiding?
★ Who are some people I am avoiding?
★ What pains am I running from?
★ How can I stop running and face each area listed?

Say Aloud: **I Feel the Pain, So I Don't Feel Regret**

Find Something You Love and Stick to It

Love comes in many forms. It's not always romantic, or parental, or friendly. Sometimes, love comes in the form of ART—our most personal TRUTH. Sometimes we express love through poetry and sometimes through the physical form of art or dance. Sometimes, love is expressed through doodling in a notebook. Sometimes, it's through oil paintings, chalk, graffiti, watercolors, spoken word, or photography.

I have dabbled in many forms of love, but oil and photography have kept me centered. When I was a child, I wasn't able to take art classes in school. My Daddy saw fit to let me take classes outside of school. Mrs. Bosch was her name. When I adopted my girls, photography became my home. I needed to capture every moment because they were new to me. Then my Mommy got diagnosed with cancer, and she affirmed for me that photography was where my art led me. Taking pictures of her during her journey of breast cancer brought us closer. She wanted every step captured, and I was there for it. She is my EVERYTHING. She not only gave me life, but she gave me purpose. I have found what I love through her eyes, and she has seen her life through mine.

In carving a bit of time out of life for yourself, take the time to involve yourself in something you love. Find your love through a form of art.

— Stephanie Hamilton Muwunganirwa

Say Aloud: I Will Find Something I Love and DO IT!

May

" I Will NOT Be Comfortably Complacent "

Loss can be construed in many different ways. There's the loss of a friend, the loss of a job, the loss of a relationship *(personal and professional)*, or a distant loved one. You can experience the loss of a pet or the loss of what you thought should have happened. *I bet you didn't realize you could feel the loss of experiences. Losing the comfortability of LIFE... I believe that's worse.* Sometimes, you are pushed so far out of your comfort zone and are at your limits of life but KNOW this: when there is a challenge in your life, you have to learn to look at it differently.

You must understand that being comfortable is different than being complacent. Understand and realize that you were equipped for GREATNESS! God made you a little uncomfortable—well, sometimes A LOT—to MAKE YOU MOVE! He has greatness in store for you, and TODAY, you can claim it, just as I and others before you have done.

★ Have you been comfortably complacent?

— Stephanie Hamilton Muwunganirwa

Affirmation Journal

★ In what areas of life have I been comfortably complacent?
★ Why am I being complacent in these areas?
★ What must I do to change my posture in this area?
★ What are the benefits of these changes?

I Will Not Be Distracted!

When you are pursuing purpose, many things will happen that could possibly get you off track. Many things happen that can distract you from your purpose. Don't allow distraction to come in from outside sources and cause you to get off task. Be mindful of internal distractions that come to your awareness and do the same thing—get you off track. Don't be caught off guard by distractions of *any* kind! They could cause you to question yourself, question your being, and question who you are all with the goal of diverting you from your goals. Don't let it happen!

When you find these patterns of mayhem occurring in your life, always remember your WHY!! Ask yourself, "Why did I start this project, and why is it important for me to stay on track to complete it?"

Beware of distractions!! Distractions are everywhere, and though you may sometimes get sidetracked and lost in the sauce, quickly get back to your tasks and block out the disruptions. Regain your focus, recalibrate your mind, and remind your heart to get back on task.

Do not be distracted because the world needs you to win!

— Coach Mechelle Canady

Affirmation Journal

- ★ Where have distractions popped up in my life?
- ★ What are they interfering with?
- ★ How can I limit these distractions so I can focus?

May 29

I Have SPECIAL Powers! 😊

We as women were created and chosen by the Most High with the ability to carry life and bring life into this world. That is a special power that only women have been given. Whether we use that power or not, we have been given innate abilities to nurture and to ensure needs are met. We must realize that these abilities were given to us for a special reason.

We have been assigned with such a great responsibility because we are equipped to handle it. So, if we can give life, surely, we can accomplish the things we aspire to accomplish, right? YEEEESS!

Because YOU have SPECIAL POWERS!!

— Erika Harp

May 30

I Am Important! I Do NOT Quit!

Right now...

...I am working on this high school diploma, and I'm trying my *hardest* to prove myself at my job. It has been a challenge, to say the least, but I know I'm GREAT. the *challenge now is convincing* them *(aka corporate America)*.

Whatever you do in life, wherever you end up, always remember God has you where you are for a purpose—for a plan. When you are feeling at your lowest, remember this: God put you in this position to do what He called you to. I mean, when you are at the end of it all and feel like you have failed, know you are better than you could ever imagine. You walk and talk like a boss, and you don't even realize your worth. You are worthy, confirmed, and committed.

Personally, I will commit to being the best woman I can be by continually holding you when you can't hold yourself. I am investing in you because YOU ARE IMPORTANT, and baby girl...
...we DON'T QUIT!

— Stephanie Hamilton Muwunganirwa

31 May

" If I Begin, I Will Win "

The hardest part of getting something done is getting started. Many times, we procrastinate and find all kinds of reasons to *not* get started. One of the greatest obstacles to getting started is the fear of failure. We fear we are going to fail; we fear we're not adequate; we even feel we can accomplish what we set out to do, and that causes us fear.

Let me encourage you here: you will *win* if you begin, so GET STARTED!!! You are a winner as long as you just get started, so figure out what you need to do and make it happen. Don't let the fear of failure cause you to fail because you never got started. Don't wait another day to get started; don't wait 'til tomorrow because tomorrow is not promised. Many good ideas have been put off 'til tomorrow, and then tomorrow never comes. So, don't be held back by the thoughts of your mind. Just Do It! Get started today because if you begin, you will win!

— Coach Mechelle Canady

Self Care!

June 1

"

SELF-Care is the Best Care!

"

For many years, I had a hard time taking care of me because I had committed all my life to helping others; I didn't want to disappoint them. After serving others without allowing servitude to be returned to me, I found myself feeling empty. Eventually, I realized I wasn't any good for those I served if I didn't become responsible enough to serve myself.

From birth to death, a woman's entire being is designed to serving others. History reminds us of countless examples of women who serve their families, partners, children, workplace mission, and visions of others, all while neglecting her own. When we focus solely on others and suppress our individual frustrations, the result is stress, anger, and feelings of low self-esteem because we feel that others are not seeing and valuing us. Know that appreciation comes first through YOU!

Beloved, I encourage you to embrace your gift of serving others and take pride in it; however, remember that SELF-care is the BEST care. Stop neglecting your own natural, spiritual, financial, social, emotional, and educational cares. Hold yourself and other women accountable to STOP—slow down and take care of SELF. Go and get that pedicure. Buy that dress. Invest in property. Take a mental health day from work. Stop explaining yourself to others and justifying your decisions through words! Put your phone on "DO NOT DISTURB!" Plan a solo trip or take a personal date night. Taking care of yourself feeds your heart, spirit, soul, and body. Learn to TAKE CARE of YOU, and then will you be able to vibrantly, cheerfully and selflessly give better care to the world.

— Regina N Roberts

Say Aloud: **SELF-Care is the Best Care!**

June 2

"This is Who I Am. I Accept My Flaws and All!"

I stare into the mirror and immediately notice all my flaws, yet I see nothing but beauty. I don't have to strive for perfection 24 hours a day, or at all if I don't care to. I have a beautiful soul that is unmatched in the love it radiates, so when I walk into a room full of beautiful women dressed in their best—their makeup is done, their hair is laid—I don't hold back from telling another, "Girl! You come to slay!" as I walk past smiling and joyful.

See, I think the very best of me because I know the very worst of me and, despite it all, I strive, I grow, I learn, I build, and I keep going with my head held high. Why? Because this is who I am. I accept my flaws and all.

— Brittany Whigham

June 3

"I Will Stay Centered"

On this journey of life, things will happen that will mess up everything you have planned. That's a fact! We have to remember that we are not exempt from anything this life can throw at us (reality check), but it's not EVER about what happens to you;

it's about how you handle what happens to you. So, when life throws you a curveball that smacks you dead in the face, consider doing the following to stay centered:

1) Pray *(Oh, Lord! Pray!)*
2) Cry, when needed *(release)*
3) Phone a friend
4) Ask yourself, "What would I tell my loved one if they came to me with this problem?"
5) Use that same advice for yourself
6) Try to get on the ball with plan B *(or C, or D, etc.)*
7) Cry some more *(if necessary)*
8) Pray some more *(It's necessary!)*
9) Be Blessed as well as a Blessing to others 😊
10) Repeat as needed *not necessarily in this order*

— Kwanza Yates

June

I Will Spend Time with ME!!!!!

Women are the pillars of their communities, the heartbeat of their families, and the masterminds behind many corporations. Women often struggle with guilt for giving others the same time, love, and attention that could be solely reserved for themselves. As women, we work hard. We carry the weight of the world on our shoulders, and we wear the complexities of others in our spirits. Today, declare to yourself, "I Will Spend Time with ME!!!!"

This affirmation serves to remind every woman to do YOU selflessly. Remember, you don't have to do it all. Be vulnerable enough to allow yourself not to have all the answers. Be open enough to allow others to help you *or* be willing to let them figure life out for themselves!

As a step toward taking care of myself, I started small and blocked out the 3rd weekend of every month for a "ME Day." the 3rd weekend is devoted to all things ME: MY business, MY personal care, MY hobbies, MY peace, and MY spirit! MY! MY! MY!

Start today. Take that weekend flight you've been considering. Go see a play at the local theatre. Read that favorite book you've read five times already. Lay in bed longer than usual. Silence your phone OR turn it off altogether! *(This is important! Life will still go on... trust me!)* Understand that you are just as important and worthy as those around you. Make a practice of giving yourself some prioritized time and make sure others do the same. Don't ask their permission. Set aside your time. *Commit* to it and ask that they follow suit. Spend time reconnecting with yourself in a quiet place on a regular basis. Spend time in meditation and prayer. No matter what you end up doing, make sure you reclaim your time!

— Regina N Roberts

June

Weekly,
I Will Remember to Take a Day for Myself

As life has become more demanding with every new venture, I've had to tackle this thing called self-care. As I've grown through life, others have always expected me to do what was considered the "right" thing. Much of that meant serving others. Over time, I started to feel guilty when I yearned to be alone or do things for myself. Most of my life, I've lived by the saying, "Not for myself, but for others," yet with the growing need for self-care, I have had to learn how to serve others in a way that didn't cause me to become bitter. Therefore, I made a conscious decision to devote time to myself even with a life that is busy and chaotic.

About three years ago, I set aside time to create a calendar of monthly events that solely served me. Serving myself meant I planned trips and took long walks in the park, amongst other things. One year, I decided to set aside the third weekend in every month of that year as "ME Day." "ME Day" required me to spend time with myself and serve myself without guilt.

In the hustle and flow of life, make sure you set aside a few minutes, several hours, or a full day to rejuvenate your core.

— Regina N Roberts

June

" I Will Take Myself Out! "

Self-care, self-love, and self-worth are key in being able to enjoy time with yourself.

Over the last 11 months, I intentionally spent lots of time with myself. This meant I traveled solo. I took myself out on dinner and lunch dates. I pampered myself by allocating the third weekend of each month to spending time with *me*. During this time, I cried. I prayed. I journaled, and I even spent hours of time resting and sleeping and listening to the silence of being still. Many times, I would reflect on the scripture that states, "Be still and know...". for a while, I didn't know what I believed that scripture to mean. Yet, over time, the value in being STILL revealed to me a sense of peace, love, and appreciation in taking myself out and loving on me.

Ladies, be intentional about taking yourself out! Explore what you like and what you don't like. Stop making assumptions about yourself based on tradition, family, and familiarity! Take that leap and try the different varieties of cuisine before you say what you don't eat. Try that new sport before you allow superstition to set in. Take a continuing education class to learn something new. Take a 15-minute walk around the track or neighborhood. Spend a little of the extra you have this month on pampering yourself. Beautify your hair or nails. Get a facial or massage or take some time for tea-time! Plan a weekend getaway and explore a new place. Journey by way of plane, train, boat, etc. and travel to a new city, state, or country. No matter what you do, remember to take yourself out! You'll be glad you did!

— Regina N Roberts

Say Aloud: **I Will Take Myself Out!**

I Will Learn How to Have A Meal Alone

It is okay to have a meal alone. Sometimes, you may need time to be alone and reflect. Doing this while having a meal is a perfect time. Whether you are in public, or in the comforts of your own home, eating a meal alone does not have to be lonely. This time can be taken to catch up on reading a book, or even to scroll what you have missed on social media.

Learning how to spend time by yourself is crucial. Learning how to be comfortable spending time by yourself is even more crucial. There may not always be someone readily available to join you for things, but the more time you spend by yourself, the more comfortable you will be with yourself.

I challenge you to have a meal alone twice a month—this is a good starting point. Ideally, this number will increase over time. There is something so relaxing about not having to carry on a conversation with others but allowing time to be spent in your own thoughts. Although it seems unconventional, it is okay to have lunch or dinner at a restaurant alone. Step out of your comfort zone and try being entertained by your company alone.

— Arielle Griffin

Say Aloud: **I Will Learn How to Have A Meal Alone**

June

" I Will Eat Right "

Say Aloud: I Will Eat Right!

But... know that consistency is the name of the game! We often think that eating right means eating salads and drinking water for as long as we can stand it, and then--when life happens--we say what the heck, I deserve this burger and fries! However, we must stop looking at eating right as dieting. Having consistent healthy habits contributes to your body's response to exercise. As you consistently eat healthier choices, the body begins healing itself which keeps risks of chronic diseases low.

The goal is to think of food as fuel. on the days you expend more energy, consume more energy... EAT! on the days you do less, eat less. There is a healthy balance for the number of calories you should consume. Not everyone needs the same number of calories. When you see related health recommendations, they are based on your activity level, and... not all calories are made equal, so keep that in mind!

Another fact to know is that you need all food groups to remain healthy, but some food groups are more beneficial than others.

Here are some tips for healthy eating:

1. Try to fill half your plate with vegetables.
2. Fill a little more than 1/3 of your plate with lean protein like chicken breast or fish.
3. Finally, fill less than a third of your plate with whole grains.
4. Eat fruits and healthy fats and oils like salmon, avocado, and olive oil in moderation.
5. Lastly, don't forget to drink plenty of water!

— Cortney D. Surrency, AC-CHC

June

I Will Take Care of My Body

You are the temple in which my soul is housed, and without you, I cannot exist. What am I?

I am the body.

I can do amazing things as long as you take care of me. with the proper nutrients, I can walk; I can talk; I can jump; I can run. I carry your children, and so much more.

Without the proper nutrients, I cannot effectively do all the things I was designed to do at my greatest capacity. Eating, sleeping, and even exercising are a few ways to keep me in top shape. These things are even proven to lead to a longer life!

I know sometimes there are not enough hours in the day to do all you need to do and still take care of yourself, but you must. Your life literally depends on how well you treat your body, so do yourself a favor. I mean… it's your life we are talking about! Remember, among all the other things in your life that matter, you matter too.

Live better.

— Chantell Williams

I Am WHOLE

Despite what you believe your limitations are, YOU, my heart, are whole. You are complete and wonderfully made. A quick scroll through a dictionary tells us that whole means *all of* something, the *entirety*. Wholeness means that something is *complete*, in itself. Whole can also be used to mean that something is *distinct* or *emphasized*. When I reviewed this, I chuckled....

Basically, a whole woman consumes three different forms of communication in the English language. A whole woman is a noun, an adverb, and an adjective all beautifully wrapped in one! Wholeness is a woman *(noun)*. Wholeness describes the woman *(adjective)*. Wholeness modifies, or even qualifies, the woman *(adverb)*! How nice!

What a gift it is to be you. You were so well thought out that you are carrying on the English language and executing it FLAWLESSLY! Haha! I'm so proud of you. Do you have any idea of the impact you have in your daily life? You were magnificently created for such GREAT purpose that there isn't even one word to describe you. We call you mother, daughter, sister, lover, friend, and so many other praises that I can't put into words. You are WHOLE and so worthy. You were made for a purpose, and in my heart of hearts, I know you and I will carry through with our calling. We will put out heads together and continue this journey of life toughing one day at a time while also not forgetting WE ARE WHOLE.

— Stephanie Hamilton Muwunganirwa

I Put Myself First

* Did you know you can't take care of others if you don't first take care of yourself?

* If you are in a bad mood all the time, if your money is always funny, if you look a mess, if you're sick all the time, if you are always unorganized, if you're hurting yourself and think negative about yourself, how can you be of any good use to anyone else?

* How can you be a beautiful example of womanhood for your children?

* How can you be a mate that is a blessing and not a headache?

* How can you be an employee that is a blessing to your organization and your coworkers and not a liability if you have not first taken care of yourself?

You can't give what you don't have. Can you loan someone ten dollars if you only have five? Can you give someone love from a place of hate? You must put yourself and your wellbeing first, so you can truly be your best for others.

— Kwanza Yates

Say Aloud: **I Put Myself First**

June

I Will Not Lose Sight of My Vision To Pursue the Visions of Others. . .

Daily, we're pulled in many directions to be of assistance to others and their goals. So much so that by the end of the day, there's no energy left for your own vision. Let's find the balance.

Similar to how we budget our money, when they say to pay yourself first, wake up and spend time with God and *your* vision first. Spend non-negotiable, unapologetic, laser-focused, intentional time on YOUR vision. Consider your vision for your life, your career, your business, your family, your health, your spirituality, and your finances. You'll find that you're a much better counterpart to those you're serving when you feel accomplished in your own life.

When you feel as though your affairs are in order, you're less stressed, and the ideas are flowing. Your mood is elevated because you've handled the important things on your end. Weights are lifted, and you can now turn your full attention to those around you. You can still be the support others need you to be, only now you're more effective and less bitter.

Amen!

Say Aloud: I Will Put My God and My Vision First.

— Monique Carter

Affirmation Journal

★ **What is my life's vision?**
★ **What visions of others gets in the way of mine?**
★ **How can I find balance between the two?**

June

I Will Understand the Essence of NO

I have learned that I cannot please everyone and that saying "no" is okay, but understanding the essence of NO is something I am still working on. If I am not feeling up to something, I am learning that it is okay to cancel plans. If someone asks me to assist with or complete a task, but I am already juggling too much on my plate, it is okay for me to say, "No."

I have a poor habit of being a people pleaser. I like those around me to be happy, and I don't like it when others are upset. It is as if I can feel negative or disappointed energy. However, I have learned that I cannot determine the happiness of others and that the only happiness I am responsible for is my own. Understanding the essence of NO is still a work in progress for me, but I have come a long way.

Overextending oneself is not good self-care. Taking time out for yourself is so necessary. If saying "no" to future obligations is the only way to take time out for yourself, then saying "no" is vital to your life.

— Arielle Griffin

Say Aloud: **I Will Understand the Essence of NO**

June

"

I Will Learn to Be Independent and Support Myself

"

I've always been an independent person. This is something my mother instilled in me at an early age. As for supporting myself—not so much.

I have worked since the age of 16, but I have not had the means to solely support myself until recently. Throughout high school and college, I have had amazing parents and family who were always available to support my financially, if needed. Unfortunately, some people are not so lucky. the "college struggle" was a real thing for me as I had to learn to budget appropriately and live off a certain amount of money—as did many of my friends. If we had not experienced this, I don't think we would have been prepared for the "real world" per se. However, once I gained a salaried job, I began to support myself independently. This was an adjustment as I had to learn to budget, save, and to have a little fun at the same time. I am still figuring these things out, but there's beauty in the process. I have learned that being independent and supporting myself is so important because these crucial skills prove to be very important in my adulthood.

—— Arielle Griffin

Say Aloud: **I Will Learn to Be Independent**

15 June

" I Will Keep Myself First "

Having balance is hard, but balance is a necessity for having a sense of wellbeing. Individuals who serve as the "giver" in relationships often struggle with keeping themselves first. the sad thing is that when a giver attempts or even just thinks about doing something for themselves, they believe they are being selfish. However, it's quite the opposite.

For you to thrive in the gift of giving, you need time to reset or recharge. If you fall out of balance, you can start to feel resentment or feel like people take advantage of you. There are two things you can do to make yourself a priority.

★ The first is to **just say no!** Setting boundaries can help save you a lot of time and even frustration. Practice lovingly saying, "No," or say, "Can I think about it?" Find that sweet spot when communicating with your loved ones.

★ Last, **schedule some "Me Time."** Get away by yourself, go for a walk, or do something you always wanted to do. If something else comes up, don't reschedule this time for yourself. Make it just as important as a meeting for work. If you don't commit to you, who will?

— Cortney D. Surreney, AC-CHC

I Will Not Overextend Myself

When you feel like you may have your hands in multiple pots and begin to feel overwhelmed, it is time to take a step back and evaluate. Yes—it's great to be involved and busy. However, what's the cost to you? Overextending yourself can lead to unnecessary stress, headaches, and anxiety, amongst other things.

I can think of many times in life when I thought I had everything under control. I was keeping up with my calendar, bills, to-do's, and everything in between. on one occasion, I felt a wave of overwhelming stress all at once. Quickly, I had to really take a step back and think of why I was so tense. After clearing my head, taking a shower, and creating a list, I was again able to think clearly.

When you are accomplishing tasks, and are extremely busy, you are not always taking the correct time to process what is happening. Even though it may seem as if you have everything in control, you might not. Overextending yourself can be dangerous to your mental health. Remember to always take care of your health—this includes both mental and physical health. Don't stress yourself unnecessarily. the result can be devastating.

—— Arielle Griffin

June

" I Will Live on a Budget "

I've heard that living on a budget shows discipline, commitment, and your power to seek delayed gratification. When you think of budgeting, money quickly comes to mind. for many, living on a budget comes with a negative connotation, while others find budgeting to be a way to maximize what's important at the right time. Living on a budget is about creating and maintaining a financially responsible lifestyle that evaluates opportunities and renders a sense of peace. Successful budgeting takes a decision to be committed and devoted to making the right choices. Budgeting doesn't just have to concern money. You can wisely choose to budget your time, spending habits, and your quality of life. It's a basic means of living within your means through mind, body, soul... and of course, through money.

Take time to reflect on your life and its current state of being. Then, identify how you will transition to a life full of healthy choices. Start small and connect with an accountability partner. Start, evaluate, and repeat.

— Regina N Roberts

This Woman's Work (Today)

★ Today, conduct a bit of research on how you can create a personal budget.
★ Take at least 30 minutes to do this.
★ Next, save some resources that will help you along the way.

This Woman's Work (This Week)

★ Spend at least 45 minutes drafting a budget.
★ Spend another 30 minutes getting all data you need.
★ Spend a final 30 minutes to make sure it all adds up!

It's Okay to Splurge Every Once in A While

For as long as I can remember, I have been frugal. I've worked since I was a teenager and have always loved to save my earnings. I have no problem spending money on others for food or gifts; however, I have had a tough time with when it comes to spending money on myself. It seems I'm always able to convince myself, "I really don't need that."

When I received my first salaried job, I spent the first paycheck on an expensive handbag. I had to convince myself that this was "okay." I've always told myself that once I began to make a living, I would reward myself with the handbag that I had always dreamed of. I decided to splurge on that material possession, and I have not regretted that decision since.

It is okay to splurge every once in a while, whether this is on yourself or on others. If I could share one piece of advice, it would be to become comfortable with treating yourself. You deserve it.

—— Arielle Griffin

Affirmation Journal

- ★ What makes me a responsible spender?
- ★ What makes me irresponsible?
- ★ How can I show myself some care with an occasional BIG purchase *(that is responsible)*?

19

June

"

I Will Find Balance

"

Physical-, mental-, spiritual-, and emotional-wellness defines your balance. This holistic approach to health is called "The 4 Quadrants of Health." Physical wellness is how you treat your physical body through your habits with nutrition and physical activity. Mental wellness is related to the health of your mind. Spiritual wellness is your belief system and emotional wellness is how you feel about yourself or your outlook on life. There are many challenges with each quadrant so it's important to have balance in each as each one depends on the effectiveness of the others. When we are lacking in one area, over time it can affect quadrants that we usually thrive in.

Conduct a self-check to see how you are doing in each quadrant.

Write down as many things as you can in 1 minute that you do well in each quadrant. If you find it tough identifying healthy habits in a particular quadrant, that could be a clear sign that you may be out of balance. You may already know that you're out of balance without doing the exercise. Either way, create goals for each quadrant and prioritize the goals within the quadrants that are lacking balance.

— Cortney D. Surrency, AC-CHC

"It's Okay to Have Days When All I Do Is. . . Chill!"

Although these kinds of days occur less often than I would like, I bask in the days where I can do absolutely nothing. I enjoy the days when I can lay in bed on a Saturday and binge-watch. Over time, I have learned that it is okay to have days where I am unproductive. I am used to being a busy body with tons of tasks on my daily calendar. However, self-care is so very important.

To some, like myself, self-care can mean taking a day to watch television and not accomplishing a thing. Your body needs a break sometimes, and your mind does as well. When I binge watch on days where I need self-care, I prefer to watch productions where I can scroll through my phone and still be able to follow along with the show. Some may call this mindless television, and I like it!

It is important not to feel guilty for taking time for yourself on lazy days. If all you do on a lazy day is sit on the couch, eat, and watch television, this is A-Okay. Lazy days are well deserved and are a necessity to keep both your body and mind healthy.

—— Arielle Griffin

Say Aloud: **It's Okay to Have Days to Just Chill!**

Girl, Get Naked! *(Censored)*

GIRL!
  Get Naked!
  Meaning…
  …be transparent!

And if you don't like what you see, either change it or change how you see it.

Getting naked can refer to unveiling the physical, financial, the spiritual—or whatever area of your life where you need to take a deep look at—and being completely transparent with yourself about what you find. How can you plan to fix what you can't even be honest about? Your transparency could take you on a journey that leads you to a fuller life and a clearer view of yourself. This transformation of yours could be a testimony of your changed life that then helps change someone else's.

GIRL!
  Get Naked!

The next transformation of your life depends on your revealing yourself to… yourself.

— Erika Harp

Affirmation Journal

  ★ What is my biggest takeaway from this post?
  ★ How can I incorporate what I learned into my life?
  ★ What is the next time that I will get naked with *me*?
  ★ What steps will I take to do this regularly?

Invest in Candles

I used to light a candle almost every day. I would burn through about three candles a month. There is something so soothing about lighting a candle and appreciating the fragrance it creates. to me, self-care can be as simple as cleaning while having a candle lit and music playing in the background. the best part about investing in candles is the enjoyment of choosing scents that align with the season. Few things compare to having your home smell like fall leaves during autumn or peaches in the spring. Lighting a candle can calm your spirit and help the unsatisfactory parts of the day to fade away. Candles can alter your entire mood and help you to have a clearer mind. Taking a bath while candles are lit can also be relaxing. These examples provide just a few wonderful ways to let go at the end of a long day. Something as simple as investing in candles can impact your day in a positive way.

Invest in candles! It will be one of the best decisions you ever make!

—— Arielle Griffin

Say Aloud: **I Will Invest in Candles.**

I Will Cry

As a child, crying was something that I did often and very easily. As I've grown through life, I've learned to curve my emotions and hold things together without letting a tear drop, yet... Crying happening at its most organic time expresses emotions, times of happiness, caution of danger, and crying helps cleanse the mind, soul, and the body. Don't let the disappointments of life, people, and wavering faith cause you to withhold a moment to cry!!! Crying is often looked upon as a sign of grief, but it can also be thought of as a form of worship.

During the most difficult seasons of life, a cousin and I would allow ourselves at least one cry a week. Somehow, we've now allowed the busy-ness of life to limit our allowance to cry. We need to learn to cry again... Cry when things are going well. Cry when new ideas begin to manifest. Cry in times of frustration. Cry when life gets overwhelmingly tough.

If you ever feel the need to, go ahead and let out a healthy cry on a regular basis! I promise you will feel loads lighter.

— Regina N Roberts

I Am A GREAT Friend to ME!

No matter what... I got me! I've got me, and I've got myself!
I'VE GOT ME!
Me, myself and I!

I am my best friend. I know myself inside and out, so I know how to take care of me. I even know that when I don't have good friends, I have myself! I know that I am good enough! I am able to be happy with me. I know that I have enough on the inside of me to be able to be successful even if the handclaps, applause, and approvals are not there. I know I have enough in me to be loved without having someone else tell me that I am enough.

I am all I need, and the greatest friend that I can have is myself. I lift myself up. I trust myself. That's what a great friend is, and that's what a great friend does. If I can't be a great friend to myself first, then I can't be a great friend to somebody else, so I am a GREAT friend to ME.

— Coach Latoya Kight

June

" I Don't Have to Deal with Everything That Comes My Way "

We aren't always who we say we are. the *"put on" has become sooooo real, and it's really sad.* I understand that everyone will not *be* to me what I have *been* to them, however...

...I do expect people to try.

When the rubber meets the road, who you are, and your purpose in my life matters. Don't just tell me what you think I want to hear! Tell me the truth and let me decide if you can stay or if you've gotta go! Instead of having a conversation with me, you have a conversation *about* me. Instead of coming to me with your concern about me you turn to others and voice it... *sigh*

Wooooosaaaaaaahhhh...

I've learned that when people mistreat you, it's not a statement of you—it's a statement of them!

How can we ever truly be honest with others if we aren't honest with ourselves first? What is it that causes us to act that way? Find the source of this issue within and take care of it!

— Chantell Williams

If You Don't Respect Yourself, No One Else Will

I always found myself exiting relationships and then wondering, 'What is wrong with me?" in high school, he said he loved me, but that just wasn't enough for him to leave his girlfriend. Despite that... I stayed... for the sake of being loved. the next one said I ruined the relationship because of my insecurities, and that was probably true. Yet again, I still wasn't enough. Now this next one, I was sure he was it. He treated me like no one ever had, even when we were just friends. So, I rushed it because I didn't want to lose him. Even after a year of perfect love, I still wasn't enough. Even after finding out I was carrying His child... I still wasn't enough.

Then...

...there was just time. A love found me that did not compare to the loves I had in the past. This relationship forced me to focus on myself more. I soon came to realize that I didn't respect myself enough for someone else to respect me. I didn't love, value, or know myself enough. How could I expect someone else to do so? This caused me to swallow a big pill: all the heartbreak I felt was a product of me not knowing who I was or how I should be loved.

We can't require of others what we can't give to ourselves. If you don't respect yourself, no one else will.

— Kenajawa LaShawn

Say Aloud: **I Will Respect Myself!**

June

I Will Take Time to Pamper Myself

As women, we are built to nurture and look after our families. We will neglect ourselves to make sure the ones we love are taken care of. When we are sick, we will keep going and fight through the illness because we know we are needed, but what about us? What about what we need? When do we rest? When do we stop and take a day to simply be?

Start today! Let's get our manicures, pedicures, and even stop to get a massage. Take yourself and your girlfriends to dinner and catch up. Go to a store and buy yourself something nice if that's in your budget. Take time to rest, so that when you wake up to be superwoman again, you aren't exhausted. Find out when the latest movie is playing that you've been anxious to see. Get yourself some popcorn and enjoy it.

The little things that we forget to do for ourselves are so important. Starting today, and going forward, promise yourself that you will take the time to simply pamper yourself. Remind your friends to do the same!

— Chantell Williams

Affirmation Journal

- ★ In what ways do I pamper myself?
- ★ What opportunities have I missed out on before?
- ★ How can I ensure my pampering happens regularly?
- ★ Who will support me in this endeavor?
- ★ What resources can I use to start my new journey?
- ★ What do I need to add to my list?

I ALWAYS Take Pride in My Appearance!

If your days don't always end up being great, get up a little early and spend some extra time fixing yourself up. Take a nice hot shower or sit down in the tub if you have that kind of time. Take your time and comb your hair in sections ensuring you have taken care of all the snags. for my ladies with short hair, you already know the drill.

Spend a couple of additional minutes on your face, whether that be with makeup or just with simple skincare. When you're done, make your way to the closet. Pick out something nice. You know… that outfit that gets you all the compliments… Yeah, that one! Put that on and find the perfect shoe and handbag to match.

No… you are not superficial. You are a precious gift to the earth. You are a light, and today, let's declare: you are a woman, and a woman, indeed you are!

Come on, ladies! Strut your stuff and always remember to take pride in your appearance.

Share this compliment of pride with the next woman you see and remind her of her power.

— Chantell Williams

Affirmation Journal

★ What steps do I take to care for my appearance?
★ What steps have I skipped in self-care in the past?
★ What top 3 things do I need to work on?
★ What kind of help do I need?
★ Who can I reach out to help with my appearance?

June

"

No More Moo Moos!!!!

"

THROW YOUR MOO MOOs AWAY LADIES!!!

Moo Moos are Noooooooooo-Noooooooooooos.

Trust me; no one loves sweats, big tee shirts, and fluffy socks more than your girl. *raises hand*

But why not prepare for bed like you prepare for the day? Why prepare and pamper to give the day your best self, but climb in bed *looking* tired? Although there will surely be days when you just do NOT care, let's not make that every day.

Bedtime is where we spend the most time with ourselves, and if you're married, it is probably the most time you spend with your spouse. Prepare yourself for bed, whether you're getting in next to someone or not. **Being sexy is for you!** Other people can enjoy the benefit as *you* so choose but prepare yourself for bed in the same manner that you prepare for the day.

Sexy yourself: soak in the tub, caress yourself in moisturizing oils, explore yourself if that's what you choose… but prepare yourself for bed and *please*…

… THROW YOUR MOO MOOs AWAY, LADIES!

Get yourself something nice and beautiful that makes *you* feel nice and beautiful!

You're never too old or young to feel pretty.

— Erika Harp

Say Aloud: **I Will TOSS My MOO MOO Out the Door!**

June

I Will Take Better Care of Myself

I'm learning more and more that people aren't always who they say they are; they aren't always who they appear to be. I'm sure you've learned this, too, or you may still be working on it, like me. Because of this, we sometimes put ourselves in complicated and uncomfortable situations when all we have to do is open our eyes. We often know from the beginning of an encounter whether the situation is good for us or not, but we willingly jeopardize our inner peace for a temporary experience. We can look at a thing, and as we see it coming, we open our heart, our mind—and sometimes our body—to it.

What is within us that makes us so naïve to what is right in front of us?

Is it our need to have things, or is it our need to prove ourselves that we can have anything we want?

Is it our brain-chatter and insecurities that make us do these off-the-wall, out of the ordinary, things that in the end leave us broken and bound?

Ladies, let's finally take the time to work on ourselves. I mean, WORK! Let's sit down and sort out the things in our lives that have caused us pain and discomfort. Let's sort through the insecurities we have because of the people we love. Let's get help if that's what it takes to be better. Let's take better care of ourselves.

I mean...

...who else will do it if we don't?

— Chantell Williams

Self
Esteem !

July 1

Self-Confidence Starts with SELF

Growing up, I did not have the greatest self-confidence. I was not comfortable with my height, my long limbs, or some of my facial features. the people surrounding me would always offer compliments to me and say phrases such as, "You just don't know how beautiful you are." I didn't understand what they meant at the time, but the older I get, I begin to have a greater understanding of my own image.

As I have grown as a person, my self-confidence has expanded extensively. I can now see the beauty in my facial features and my height. I am no longer afraid to wear heels in fear of being even taller than I already am.

I gained most of my self-confidence in college. This was a huge period of growth for me as a person. However, for eighteen years, I had walked through life with sub-par self-confidence. I did not have strong self-confidence until I began to see my outward and inner beauty.

Others can tell you that you are beautiful all day and all night. Sadly, this does not mean a thing until you can believe it yourself. You are beautiful.

— Arielle Griffin

Say Aloud: **Self-Confidence Starts with SELF**

July 2

I Like Who I Am

I hope you are one who was fortunate enough to have a mom or another adult in your life who was an encourager. As the oldest of five girls, my mom's gift was figuring out *our* gifts. I was always told to do my best, and if one of us didn't understand something, we were told to simply ask for clarification. Who we were as individuals then has definitely played out for who we are now, for who I am.

I like who I am... a caretaker, mom, a mom figure, planner, a creator, cook, an organizer, the house executive, and one who's always seeking growth within. Sometimes, I wonder why I've been blessed so with being the person I'm continually growing to be? God has been good to me, and I like who I am!

Through finding ways to pass on to others what you know, you will grow to respect and like yourself even more.

— MommyV

July 3

I Love My Skin

Chocolate, honey, molasses, cocoa brown, milk chocolate, caramel-colored, latte, espresso, and the list could go on...

I am describing my skin tone.

I love it. I **BIG** LOVE IT!

It is beautiful, but more than the tone, I love the skin I'm in. the skin I am in includes the tone, but it is also the way I stand, walk, and sit in my identity as me. It is the first thing you see when you glance in my direction. Loving my skin means not doubting myself because I am affirmed when I appear. Loving my skin means walking confidently, boldly, brilliantly in the significance of who I am and what I—and the collective—bring to the table. the contribution is priceless!

When I look in the mirror—the soul reflector—I see sun-kissed style, trendsetter, phenomenal essence, sassy classy, innovator, the creativity, social commentator and demander of justice, the breath of fresh air, resilient in nature, smooth, but sometimes prickly in texture, always interesting, intriguing, and mysterious.

I love MY skin; it is rich, though hidden, and history proclaims I AM HERE to STAY.

— Dr. Latisha D. Reeves Henry

July

"

I Love My Hair

"

A woman's hair is a sense of strength, love, identity, status... and stress! the transformation of a woman's hair exemplifies where she may be in life or where she hopes to be displaying her innermost emotions. Just as with a growth process in life, a woman's hair tells a story of nurturing, growth, captivity, and freedom.

At the age of 24, I decided to cut my hair to a length that rested around my earlobe. This experience was provoked by emotions that were escalated by a sense of suffocation. Then, a few years later, I decided to wear my hair in its natural state. to accomplish this natural state of my hair, I decided to cut my hair again; this time, I cut my hair really reeeeaaally short. This cutting of my hair created a clean slate. I no longer felt bound by the demand to schedule salon visits and the repeated need for hair oils, lotions, or other potions.

During that period in life, I was transitioning—yet again—into a new dimension of my life, and I expressed all of what I was feeling through the cutting of my hair. That time around, I also explored various colors. My most fulfilling hair color experiment was when I became a redhead one summer. the red hair color showed sass, growth, and it exemplified a bold step into womanhood.

Mood is expressed through the cut, style, shape, color, coil, and curl of a woman's hair. What does your hair say about you?

— Regina N Roberts

July

I Love My Lips!

As far back as I remember, one of my nicknames within my family was "Louie lips" because I have always had such full lips. Although this was meant to be a good-natured dig, for most of my childhood, I hated my lips. I would feel self-conscious when I smiled and would often cover my mouth because of my huge lips—*such a negative feeling about such a small part of me.*

At some point, I had to learn to appreciate my lips; this wasn't an overnight process. I had to learn to accept my lips... *and to accept them on my face!* Some may see them as an imperfection. Perhaps, they just are a bit too full but combined along with every other aspect of me, they make up this perfectly unique individual.

I love my lips...

...exactly as they are.

— Brittany Whigham

I Love My HIPS!!!

I love my hips!

Just as we attribute the heart to being the house of the soul, so too does that hip play a major role in supporting the human body. It is our hip that provides support for the weight of the body during standing, walking, and running.

Ladies... whether you have big hips, small hips, lots of hips, or limited hips, your hips support the weight of life as you walk *(and run)* through life's journey. Consider your hips as supporting you in standing on the foundation you build to succeed! Embrace your hips no matter their size, shape, and function and find the joy in all that your hips help bring forth... like babies!!!

Big hips or small hips... whether walking, running, or standing... make it a practice to love your hips!

— Regina N Roberts

I Am GREAT!

When is the last time you looked at yourself in the mirror and said something positive to yourself?

We so often look at the lives of others and think, "They are really great." We look at what others have and what they do, and we think, "They have a great life." We compliment what they have, yet when is the last time you complimented yourself? When is the last time you said something sweet to yourself for encouragement?

It is great to encourage yourself, because, of course... you are great!!! Not only are you great, but you're mighty and powerful, and you have everything that you need to leave a footprint of greatness in the earth.

Once you understand that you are great, you will command the things around you to express that same greatness. Greatness lives within! with all that is in you, you can be that next boss, that fancy entrepreneur, or even be that mentor to another woman who needs to see her own greatness.

Greatness lives on the inside of you, so go to your mirror and tell yourself, "You're great!"

Tell yourself this daily because you *are* great every single day!

— Coach Mechelle Canady

July

No One Else Can Compare to ME!

Before great ideas and visions begin, a simple thought comes to mind. Sometimes, when these plans come to mind, we begin to compare our vision to the outcomes of others. We compare our thoughts to what we see on social media. We compare our planned successes to the failures of others. When we get to the point of believing in who we are, we understand that there is no measure—nor is there is a ruler—that can measure us according to our own abilities. We are unique individuals. There is no one like us! Who can we compare ourselves to?

What are you comparing yourself to? Is it the thought of another's gift or the thought of their ability? to compare yourself to others is like comparing horses to unicorns. You are uniquely made, and when God made you, he broke the mold. When God gifted you, he gave your skills to no one else. Only you can bring to the world what you have been set out to do. Only you can bring to the world what you are destined to do, so don't compare yourself to anyone.

You are beautiful and wondrously made. There is no one in the world who can beat you being you. Embrace who you are and don't compare yourself to the likes of others because there is no one who measures up to you. No one else can compare!

— Coach Mechelle Canady

July

" I Am FIERCE! "

I walk with my head held high because that's what my grandmother taught me! Whenever I leave my house, I am well put together because that's what my parents taught me. "Never leave home looking like you are not a kept woman because a first impression is a lasting impression." Don't *you* like to be doted on? I do!

When I compliment another woman on her outfit, I am extending confidence. I'm letting her know, "Girl, I see you, and you look good!" I graciously give a compliment, not looking for one in return, but simply to be a reminder for that woman... for that day. I am in every way my sister's keeper, and if I can shine some light on her for just a moment, I have done my job for the day.

"You have a beautiful smile!"

"Your hair is really pretty."

"I love the way you put that outfit together."

"Your makeup is the bomb!"

"Those shoes are to die for!"

Are you smiling yet? Well, you should be, so do me a favor! the next room you walk into, channel these compliments, and give them out to a sister or two.

Oh, and when you walk into that room today... OWN IT because sister, you are fierce!

— Chantell Williams

July

I Will Walk with CONFIDENCE

Walk with confidence...
This means to walk standing up straight, looking ahead,
    and holding your shoulders back
Walk with a purpose...
    Walk like you know where you are going...
    and why you are going there...
Others can sense low self-esteem when people don't walk
    confidently
Walking with confidence can help increase your self-
    esteem
The way you walk can speak volumes
Not that you care too deeply about what others think
    about you,
    but walking with confidence can cause you to look
    like you are prepared and have a handle on things
Show others that you are confident by holding your head
    high... avoid slouching
When going in for a job interview—
    or even while shopping at the mall—confidence is
    exerted when you look ready to conquer the world
Don't continue to waste time dealing with low confidence
The time to change is NOW

— Arielle Griffin

Say Aloud: I Will Walk with CONFIDENCE!

I Will Not Be Ashamed of Where I Came From or What I Have Experienced

One thing I have always heard is, "Never forget where you came from." It is a phrase often spoken to those who are advancing, or who have already advanced, to a certain "status." Community elders once told us these things so that we would not be ashamed of where we once lived or of those who still live there. Life lessons were learned, giftings were discovered, and they were cultivated with acknowledgment of this advice. Despite the community dysfunction, abandoned buildings, drug addicts, prostitutes, projects, or the outwardly beautiful manicured lawns masking houses of perversion and abuse... we were nurtured and matured in those old homes where we came from. We need not wear the shame of someone else's actions and things we could not control. Shame is a burden that is never ours to carry. No matter where we started or how we were forced to live, our greatest proclamation TODAY is... THAT is in the PAST! Chronologically, it is in the past, and mentally... it is in the past, so LET IT GO!

It is up to us to disarm the past of its power to overwhelm, sabotage, control our emotions, and dictate our future. We are not the sum of the things that have happened in our lives. NOW is the time to free ourselves to live as standard-bearers. Let us show other women that it is *fully* possible to overcome by *choice*.

Stop being ashamed of your past. Walk with the knowledge that YOU are more than a conqueror. Walk in grace, walk in authority, and walk in power, never being ashamed of where you have come from or what you have experienced.

— Dr. Latisha D. Reeves Henry

July

I Live in Truth

In understanding what it meant to live in truth, I had to realize what it meant to become true to myself. Before, I was living a total lie. of course, before becoming saved, I lived in sin—that's evident. After learning myself, in Christ, I realized my entire life was a lie. I lived doing the things I thought others wanted me to do. I did things I thought others liked. I really did not know myself at all. And, if I am honest, I am still learning myself to this day.

The difference between now and then is that these days, I can live in my truth, and live in it freely. My truth does not equal perfection: I am still a mess. I will still mess up, but the difference now is that I realize that all those things are a part of my message. And no matter how tainted my message seems, it still matters, and it's still MY TRUTH!

So, ladies, it's time that we live in our truth no matter how the truth sounds when it comes out!

Live in your truth and live in it freely.

— Kenajawa LaShawn

Affirmation Journal

- ★ **What is MY TRUTH?**
- ★ **Why is my truth so important to me?**
- ★ **Why is my truth so important for me?**
- ★ **Who else needs to know my truth?**
- ★ **How have I, or how will I, share my truth with them?**

July 13

"

I Will Be HONEST with MYSELF

"

We all have flaws. It is no secret that no one is perfect, but why is it so hard for many of us to realize and confront our own faults? Instead of facing ourselves, we often opt for denial and a false sense of confidence or superiority. We get defensive or argumentative anytime someone tries to call us out on our mess. This is unhealthy for any relationship. Instead of opposing the true views of those who love us, we should strive first to have a healthy and honest relationship with ourselves.

Truth is one of the most important steps to our personal growth and development. If multiple people say the same thing about you, it may be time to take a step back and self-evaluate. Do people say you are selfish? Look into your actions. Perhaps there is something within you that you truly need to work on. That's not to say everything everyone says about you is even relevant, but if you notice a negative pattern in close relationships with a common theme, then perhaps it's time to look within.

— Brittany Whigham

I Will No Longer Hide

From within, I shine,
not always letting my light reach the surface of my
       skin, but I can feel it on the inside.
I constantly speak to the inner parts of my being,
       letting her know it's almost time.
It's almost time for the light to reach my surface and
       penetrate through my skin.
At that moment, I will be free from me.
Free from worry and my own mind that told me I wasn't
       ready or that someone else can do it better.
Free from my own fear of inadequacy that was
       created the first time I failed at anything.
Free from what they told me I could not be or could
       not do.
I finally allowed the light to be me,
       and that's the moment I stopped hiding.

— Chantell Williams

July
15

I Will Stop Letting My Talents Go Unused

There is nothing worse than having gifts and talents that you don't use. These are God-given gifts and abilities...

...and you sitting on them *insert several sits!!!* it's almost like being disobedient to God when you are not using the gifts and talents that you were blessed with.

Maybe your disobedience is why you're not where you desire to be in your journey.

Stop letting your talents go unused!

— Erika Harp

16

July

"

I Am A Creator

"

Each of us was created in the very image of God. Born in relationship to all of humanity, we were given dominion over all as stewards. What an awesome responsibility and privilege!

Being made in the image of the Creator means we have been given a measure of creativity according to who we are and how we are to have an impact in the earth. Sisters, we are creators because there is something filtered through the unique beauty and creativity of each one of us. It yields a treasure specific to our different experiences and perspectives. Our lives and works are a woven tapestry, priceless, essential contributions from God through us.

I create because I am a designer's original. I birth and bring forth phenomenally by divine design. the only limit to my productivity is unbelief or limited imagination—both of which I adamantly decline. I intend to leave the world a masterpiece for God's glory.

I was born to create and that I will.

— Dr. Latisha D. Reeves Henry

17

July

" I Will Do What I Love "

Everyone talks about how important it is to find your passion.

If you do what you love, you never work a day in your life.

Marc Anthony

The reality is that loving what you do is work. the difference is you react more positively to struggles, failure, and other obstacles when you are doing what you love. Yes, it's important to follow your passion, but identifying your passion is the first step to doing work that you love.

You're probably saying, "How do I find passion?" Passion can be found through doing the things you're really good at or through simply using a strength that you possess. Maybe you are good with your hands, musically inclined, awesome with children, or artistically creative. While these are skills that we can easily identify as hard skills, think about the things that you naturally do well. Soft skills can be your biggest asset!

Whenever I would meet with a leader in my industry, they would always ask me, "What do you love doing?" I'd say, "I know I love people." (lol) I would downgrade my strengths because I didn't feel they had quantifiable value. However, soft skills--like being able to influence others, build relationships, problem-solve, see the big picture or pull out potential in others--can all assist you with identifying your passion. It's not always about being an expert in something or having a hard or technical skill that can get you to purpose. It's about identifying your natural gifts and using them with confidence!

Today, start writing down things that interest you and things that you are naturally good at. Whatever you write down, trust it, and start improving your strengths--stop focusing on your weaknesses. Why not spend your valuable time getting great at something you naturally do well!

— *Cortney D. Surrency, AC-CHC*

18

July

I Am Growing Educationally

Growth is an indication of living and thriving. A willingness to grow causes us to increase our capacity to receive and to give. Education is one of the more systematic approaches to learning, yet no matter the source of our learning, it is up to us to personally commit to our own advances of knowledge.

I remember when I first discovered that I love learning. I was in a challenging master's degree program surrounded by Caucasian males who had determined that I should not be studying in the particular track I had chosen because I was a female. I was intimidated. Through the hardship, God helped me to get understanding. the dots were connecting. I was called to this increase, and I soon found that education was the catalyst. It was part of God's provision for my expansion of knowledge, and God has given me the capacity to advance in education to deliver sound doctrine and scriptural truth.

One I learned that, education was no longer an inconvenient thing to be dreaded or avoided. in the past, it had been my vehicle to a better life for my daughter and I, now, however, purpose was attached. My continued educational pursuits silenced the critics, and the title of doctor has been rewarding.

Seize and enjoy opportunities to grow educationally. It paves an endless pathway for you to grow, bear fruit, and to impart to others so that they, too, develop a love of knowledge along with their capacity to receive and give. Education produces options, and... we like options.

Yes. We are growing educationally, whether formally at an institution, less formally in a community program, or from a dynamic leader or trainer. We are always educationally growing.

— Dr. Latisha D. Reeves Henry

July

I Am Growing Professionally

As a professional in any industry, there are certain trends, best practices, and educational credentials you are required to obtain. Professionals are also expected to have close connections with others to get their jobs done—we maximize on these connections to be successful.

Grow as a professional. Make new friends. Educate yourself. Be open to learn and grow through the trends. Set a standard and shape your brand. Be sure of who you are and all you have to offer. Trust the process, knowing that your journey will move at a different tempo, but every step will be valuable. Be clear about your self-worth, your value, and your skillset. As a professional, be clear about your BIG picture. Be intentional about the people you are connected to and the purpose of your connection. Be mindful of the unknown, unseen and unheard. Never step on the backs of others to get to the top, but always GROW despite the obstacles you will surely face along the way.

— Regina N Roberts

I Am PROUD of My INDEPENDENCE

As a teenager, my mom was always asking me to help by running errands and getting tasks done. These errands ranged from paying bills to grocery shopping to returning items, and other tasks. I did not realize how much running these errands benefited me in the long run until recently. A close mentor pointed out that by running these errands—whether intentionally or not—my mother was teaching me independence. Through running errands, I learned how to pay property taxes, shop using coupons, multitask, handle deadlines, and much more. I am proud of this independence because I have learned how to manage my own affairs.

When I left for college, I was more likely to handle problems or situations on my own, rather than calling home. I felt I could handle these things because I was comfortable doing so.

Be proud of your independence. Take on new challenges knowing that you can handle anything you put your mind to.

—— Arielle Griffin

Say Aloud: **I Am PROUD of My INDEPENDENCE**

I Am My Own Confidence Booster

I push myself.

Period.

I don't need anyone else to tell me that I'm great. I don't need anyone else to tell me that I'm beautiful. I don't need anyone else to tell me that I'm amazing. I believe it on my own.

I boost myself. I believe in myself. I love myself. If no one ever says it, if no one ever sees it, I know that all the good I believe about myself is there.

God is giving me the confidence in knowing that I am amazing just by being ME. I am amazing because He created me, so if I continue to believe and speak life into myself, I will be okay. I don't have to worry about whether anyone else is going to agree because I know that everybody may not see my truths, and that is okay. Everybody may not know my essence, yet as long as I know it, and I believe what God said about me, I will be fine, and my confidence will continue to soar.

I cannot afford to believe all the negative things that others have said about me. the truth is, no one will ever be able to tell me that I'm any different than what I believe I am. That is why I MUST believe the BEST about me always and in all ways.

I am true to who I am. I believe in who I am. I am so confident that it doesn't matter who else agrees. I don't need anyone else to validate me: I validate myself. God validates me, so my confidence soars.

My confidence lives in a high place because I believe what God has created me to be, so

I push myself.

Period.

— Coach Latoya Kight

I Will NOT Succumb to Low Expectations of Me

Have you ever had someone think they have you all figured out? Maybe you're quiet. Maybe you keep to yourself, and because their personality doesn't vibe with yours, they make assumptions about your character, about what you're like—they assume that you're weak. They are wrong!!!

I will not succumb to another's low expectations of me because they don't know me and whether they get the opportunity to know me, or not, is 100% my liberty to allow.

See, everyone isn't influential enough to know the real you, to let into your bubble, or to let into your space. Keep your head up and understand, my love, that you owe no one an explanation for who you are at your core. You are great, and it shows in how you care for people and how you allow people to have their own opinions; you are an ally for the voiceless. You take a stand for what is right, even when it isn't the popular stance. Even when the risk is high, you consciously do the moral thing. By knowing what God has called you to, you also know that the impression you have of yourself is far more important than anyone else's impression of you. They are glancing from the exterior point of view using their own life experiences to construct, and sometimes project, their feelings of self onto you because you carry a quality they lack. Don't let their views minimize you. Do not succumb to their low expectations. They do not have you figured out.

— Stephanie Hamilton Muwunganirwa

My Life Is A Testimony

For most of my life, I found myself questioning why I went through some of the things I did. Why did my parents abandon me at such a young age? Why did I struggle through college? Why didn't I have the support my peers did after becoming an adult? Why was I raped? Why did I lose my child? It wasn't until I realized that the trials I endured would help others see the glory of God, that I realized... **MY LIFE IS A TESTIMONY!**

My favorite scripture, Genesis 50:20 says, "You intended to harm me, but God intended it all for good. He brought me to this position, so I could save the lives of many people." This scripture changed my perspective on life. It felt good knowing that all the "bad" I went through would help to save others' lives. From giving birth to a stillborn child at age 20 to failing my first year of college and not being able to graduate because I owed the school money... And there are OH so many heartbreaks in my fall from God over a man...

In everything we endure, there is a lesson, and those lessons that we learn are meant to be shared with others to help them see God's power. No matter where you are in life right now, remember that your story will later be used to show God's glory.

Your life is a testimony.

— Kenajawa LaShawn

My Life Is A Blessing

Feeling that your life is anything less than a blessing has everything to do with your perspective on life. in the times when I felt like my life was not worth living, it was because my perspective on life was skewed. God has shown me, in multiple ways, that my life is a blessing. This can only be true, but I attempted to end my life five times, and each time, it was like God was saying, "I didn't tell you to do that. I still have work for you to do." for a long time, I did not see my life as a blessing. I honestly saw it as a curse. I hated living and just could not understand why I was here.

Then, God revealed to me my gift: my words. He showed me how my writing could impact and change people's lives, and I realized I was special. Every trial I had endured was intentional. My best friend always tells me, "You're going through what you are going through because, without it, you would not have a story to tell." I hold on to that because I realize that the things I am going through are not for me at all, but for the saving of someone else. What better blessing is that?! Therefore, you must remember that your life is a blessing as well!

— Kenajawa LaShawn

Say Aloud: **My Life Is A Blessing!**

"Suicide is NOT an Option!"

Thoughts of suicide flowed through my mind continually. My husband had left me, and I was unemployed with two girls. Daily, the thought of suicide seemed better and better. As a Christian, I wrestled with it in my mind, and I could not get past my circumstances. More than anything, I was just tired—tired of simply wanting someone to love me like I loved them.

There was no magical pill that changed my mind. There was no counseling. All there was were my two girls. I had to regroup and make a life for them. It took time, but I learned to appreciate the small things in each day. for every job I didn't get, I would tell God thank you for the experience I received in each interview. in time, I had a job and a new place to live.

I learned to love me and stop waiting on someone else to validate me. I recovered from the divorce and all the debt that followed. in time, I remarried a WONDERFUL man. We are now celebrating 24 years together, and I am so glad I realized long ago that...

...suicide was not an option.

Freda Wells

Affirmation Journal
★ Have I ever considered thoughts of suicide?
★ Am I considering such thoughts now?
★ What are the resources available to me (or others)?

July

I Remember My Worth

I have high self-esteem, not in a cocky way, as if I don't think I'm capable of mistakes. Rather, I have high self-esteem in a way that helps me know I am capable of whatever I put my mind to. Now, granted, I may not always "put my mind" to things in the most productive way, but... man, oh man, when I do!!! I am focused on the task at hand, and it is on AND POPPIN!!!

When I think about the things that I didn't pull myself out of, and some of the unnecessary hurt I experienced, I realize that God made an amazing woman. He covered me when I wasn't able to cover myself. He pulled me out of situations that could have been so much worse, and He is doing the same for you now.

He is carrying you even when you think he's forgotten about you, so remember your worth. God values you, so you can walk into any room with your head held high, knowing who you are and whose you are.

There is nothing you can't do when you put your mind to it.

— Stephanie Hamilton Muwunganirwa

Say Aloud: **I Remember My Worth**

When I Look Good, I Feel Good!

Usually, when reading articles or statistics about the importance of appearance, the focus is on how you dress. While how you dress and present yourself to the world is very important, this topic could be debated for hours and hours. Let's look at this in a different way. Close your eyes and think about when you're having a bad day. What's the expression on your face? What's your posture? Are you standing up straight or slouching? Did you look like you wanted to get out of bed that day? How you feel can drive facial expression, body language, and how you dress.

Life isn't always peaches-and-cream, and you are entitled to have bad days. However, consistently having an appearance of defeat can attract a whole lot of negative vibes your way. You could attract negative people, miss out on opportunities to improve your situation, or you could get a reputation of being the negative Nancy! So, while dressing for the part is a must, having a posture of friendliness, confidence, determination, resiliency and positivity will shine through brighter than any 3-piece suit ever will. Always remember, when you feel good, you look good, and when you look good, you feel good!

— Cortney D. Surrency, AC-CHC

I Am Amazingly Delightful

The dictionary has defined wondrously as something *amazingly delightful*. Accordingly, Psalms 139:14 declares, "I praise you because I am fearfully and wonderfully made, your works are wonderful, I know that full well." the writer is praising the Lord, for the Creator has made him beautiful and amazing. Consider everything God made in Genesis 1. At the end, God said, "That is good," and that is exactly what God says about you!

God created you, and you were not a mistake. You were not made by chance. You were designed and crafted by a master who loves you and cares for you so much that he made you WONDERFUL! God made you beautiful; He made you wondrous! He made you... *amazingly delightful*, so stop doubting your purpose. Stop doubting your beauty because there is no one like you. There is none created under the heavens or on the earth who is like you. Look at your hands, look at your feet, look at your face... There is no one who can compare to the beauty that is YOU! You... are wonderful. You... are beautiful, and since you were wondrously made, you were created in the image of a beautiful, wonderful, and amazing God. SO...

Walk there... in the beauty of His holiness. Walk in the beauty of who you are. You are the only creature who was created like you. Don't look to the left! Don't look to the right! Look down on the inside of you because you are amazing, you are beautiful, and you are fearfully and wonderfully made!

— Coach Mechelle Canady

"

I Will Respect Myself

"

I Will Respect Myself...
  By acknowledging my strengths and weaknesses.
I Will Respect Myself...
  By being authentic and free.
I Will Respect Myself...
  By providing my heart, mind, soul, and body with opportunities that are deserving.
I Will Respect Myself...
  By taking care of me, having patience, and living a healthy life.
I Will Respect Myself...
  By being mindful of the things I expose myself to.
I Will Respect Myself...
  By learning about my ancestry and embracing who I am.
I Will Respect Myself...
  By setting standards, upholding them, and not being afraid to stand out.
I Will Respect Myself...
  By giving myself permission to cry, ask for help, speak up, share, and say no without regrets.

I Will Respect Myself!

— Regina N Roberts

This Woman's Work (Today)

★ Using the same writing pattern listed above, write out 5 examples of how you already respect yourself.

★ Start with, "I Respect Myself By..."

★ Using the same writing pattern listed above, write out 10 examples of how you *will* respect yourself.

★ Start with, "I *Will* Respect Myself By..."

"

I Am Enough

"

One day, I stumbled across this video titled, "I am enough." the creator of the video shared the great gains and successes that she has had as a life coach through the power of simply getting people to believe that they are enough.

Living in a society where we are ranked according to our peers from the time we are born until the time we die generates the idea that who we are and where we are, just simply isn't enough. in this day and age of social media where we see into the lives of others, it's easy to measure yourself against the life of someone else without knowing if what they show you is totally true or not. the pictures don't tell you what others had to do to get to where they are.

Watching that video made me think about the way I see myself. I took a sticky note and put it on the mirror in my bathroom; I wrote on that sticky note, "I Am Enough!" Whenever I come in contact with people who struggle with their identity, I say to them, "You Are Enough!"

When we begin to deeply believe in our gifts, our talents, and our ability, we will have an impact on others.

I encourage you to look in the mirror daily, and say to yourself, "I Am Enough!" Write it on the wall. Write it on your mirror. Post it on your desk. Put it in your phone and everywhere else that you can see until you are *convinced* that YOU ARE ENOUGH! Once you start believing you are enough, others will also accept that you are enough. You will believe in yourself. You will strive to be the best version of yourself, and fear will have to cease because you will no longer be afraid to be who you are because YOU... ARE... ENOUGH!

— Coach Mechelle Canady

Say Aloud: **I Am Enough!**

July

" I Am #1 "

I am # 1 means I am choosing to FOCUS on ME... one day at a time... one moment at a time... celebrating victories at every phase of life... and getting clear with who I am. Learning who I am and what I want. I am #1... discovering who I am BECOMING.

I am #1 means to spend time with YOU! Putting yourself first means to have a preference and to go with it at all costs. It means to walk with a stride of confidence, poise, and grace. It means adorning yourself with inner jewels, clothing yourself with self-love and self-worth, and endowing spaces of life with vulnerability.

You are #1!

— Regina N Roberts

Affirmation Journal

★ What does it mean to be #1?
★ How can I work through the discomfort of being #1?
★ How do I show myself that I am, in fact, #1 in my life?
★ How can I get others to support this affirmation of me?

Say Aloud: **I Am Enough!**

Self Love!

August 1

"

I Am in LOVE with ME!

"

I love every inch of me!

I don't know why so many think that the love they have for themselves should come from outside approval and acceptance. **Chile!** I don't care who doesn't like me! I love me some ME! I don't claim to be a perfect person, but I am an awesome one! I will hype myself up in a room full of opposition. I am forever growing and evolving as a woman, and I have fallen head over heels for this beautiful soul I am becoming. I make mistakes, but I learn. I may fail, but I don't give up. I am so confident in myself and my abilities, **and why shouldn't I be?** I have breath in my lungs, so I am still working to become the most perfect me I can be, and honey, I am in love with ME.

— Brittany Whigham

August 2

"

I Have SURVIVED! I Am Built to Last!

"

As I sit here and think about everything that I've been through in life, I remember how I've been able to overcome it all! I am victorious because I have a victorious God that keeps on keeping me and guiding me. I've survived many seasons of brokenness! I've been tired! I've been depressed! I've been used, mistreated, unappreciated, mishandled, taken for granted, lied to, lied on, and let down, but I have SURVIVED! I was rebuilt! I was reborn! I have been remade. I was literally put back together each and every time I felt broken! Now, I sit in great anticipation for what is to come! My trial didn't overtake me. My broken heart didn't break me! I am so strong! Wow!

I AM SO STRONG! I AM HIGH QUALITY! I AM VIRTUOUS! I AM STRENGTH WRAPPED UP in LOVE! I AM HER--SHE WHO IS MADE in the IMAGE of GOD, HER FATHER WHO HOLDS the WORLD in the PALM of HIS HANDS NEVER FORGETTING I AM BUILT to LAST AND WITHSTAND the TEST of TIME!

Trust!
Trust, baby girl!
You are SO close!

— Chantell Williams

August

Don't Break! Break THROUGH!

On your life's journey, there will be difficult times. I read once that failure is a productive part of success. the journey of success will include both highs and lows. Stay encouraged; discouragement can create depression, and depression can develop into a defeated spirit. During the lows, some of your most unique and authentic character traits are revealed and fostered: creativity, relationship building, time management, self-development, etc. Consider the lows as a time of being planted, deeply rooted under the soil, receiving all the vital nutrients needed to grow and produce a plentiful crop. So...

On your journey of life, know that your ability to break through is your defining moment.

Don't break.

Break through.

— Erika Harp

August

"

I Am a WARRIOR! I Am Not a Victim.

"

Anyone who knows me knows I don't mind sharing my story to help others. My stories are my testimonies. They have made me who I am. I was molested twice at a young age. I had a baby in college, yet I finished my bachelor's and went to get my master's. I suffered from depression, mental abuse, cervical cancer, was divorced, was raised in a broken family, am a single mom, and I am a survivor of stage three breast cancer; this doesn't define who I am. All this says is I am a fighter, and I value life, my kids, my happiness, and my peace of mind.

I know things aren't always going to be great, but such is life. Amid every situation I've been in, I've always been concerned about others more than myself.

Today, I urge you to take care of self. At least once a day, do something that makes you smile. It could be as simple as sitting outside, watching the clouds pass for 5 mins. Do it! You deserve it!

In facing cancer for a second time, I fought a fight that has truly changed my mindset.

Learn to be honest with yourself. Share the truth of your stories. Then, you can be honest with others, and they can share the truth of theirs!

— Monique Denise

I Am Strong

I Am Strong when
I can consider others before myself,
I am strong when
I see other in need and lend a helping hand,
I am strong when
I am able to love those
who can't love me back.
I am strong because
I can encourage someone else
when they aren't able to help themselves.
I am strong when
being myself and having hope to become a better
me through sharing my trials and triumphs.
I am strong in my ability to be patient
with others,
to listen to others,
and to not judge others.
I am strong in my efforts
to help others through deeds.
I Am Strong.

— Carolyn E. Thompson

I Am PROUD to Be ME!

When was the last time that you felt truly proud of yourself or your accomplishments? Has it been a while since you have taken the time to show yourself some appreciation? Why is that?

Why do we often put ourselves at the bottom of the list? We show our love and appreciation to everyone else, but often forget to even acknowledge ourselves and all that we do.

Today, take a step back. Look at all that you do and accomplish--the big and the small. Even if you struggle, or even if you sometimes want to quit, be proud of everything that you have accomplished and continue to push through. You deserve that much.

Too often, we think we must make it to the finish line first before we celebrate ourselves, and that shouldn't be the case. Be proud of you, every step of the way. Remember, life is a physical process that requires spiritual progress. Be proud of your progress wherever you may be on that path because you are still further along today than you were on yesterday.

— Brittany Whigham

Say Aloud: **I Am PROUD to Be ME!**

August

I Make SELF-LOVE a Priority!

Staring in the mirror, I embrace all that is me. I can feel the love that I exude, and I smile. According to "them," I need braces, but I like my smile, just as it is. I have my father's smile encased behind my mother's full lips. I am my own biggest fan. Now that I am head over heels in love with ME, I am always rooting for me instead of doubting me. My very first true love was myself. It wasn't until I truly learned how to love myself that I was fully capable of loving others. *Self*-love is the best love.

A few years ago, following the birth of my daughter, my weight ballooned to be far too heavy for my 5'2 frame. My body ached from the neglect, but for the longest time, I was in denial. I ate horribly, I didn't work out, and as the numbers on the scale crept higher and higher. to solve the problem, I just went shopping. New, bigger clothes covered me from the truth. I was not healthy, and I was not happy with myself. This self-construed gimmick worked for some time, but at some point, I had to wake up and realize that I wasn't taking care of me properly. I didn't love me correctly, and that in itself was a learning process that started with taking care of *me* and *my* needs first.

I had to start being good to my mind, my body, and my spirit. I started eating better, and I cut out so much fast food. I started moving more. I don't have a lot of "free time," but wherever I go, I try to be sure to just get up and move. I take a quick walk. I do jumping jacks. I do squats, and just about anything that helps me become a better me all around.

Since making these changes, I've dropped quite a bit of weight. Still, more importantly, I feel great, and I understand the importance of making self-love a priority.

When you are good to you, you improve your mood, and you attract good, so good things happen. Be sure to show yourself some self-love in whatever way you may need. You owe it to yourself to love yourself without exception.

— Brittany Whigham

August

What Others Think of Me Matters, Just Not as Much as What I Think of Myself

I wake up in the morning, shower, brush my teeth, apply my makeup, and figure out what I am going to wear. I step out of the house fresh to death and look for a compliment just to be sure I chose right. If no one says anything, I try again the next day, and so on, until I get it right.

The problem with this process is that I run the risk of always trying and seemingly getting it wrong in the eyes of others.

Everything you do concerning you has to be done for you, or you will always be people-pleasing--you will always be at the mercy of people and what they think is the standard for you. You must be able to look at yourself and say, "This is good," or "I look great," even if no one else says a word.

They say self-love is the best love, but that's only true if you believe it. Do you believe it?

— Chantell Williams

August

"

To Thine Own Self Be True.
Don't Pay Too Much Mind
to What Others Think or Do.

"

To thine own self be true

Don't pay too much mind

To what others think or do

This affirmation is probably the hardest to hold on to

But how can I be true to you, if I am not first true to me

I admit it took me a while to realize

That the opinions of others, really hold no weight

I no longer can allow your perception to distort my
   worldview

This loving, caring heart, for a long time, was only
   committed to you

But myself I neglected for the sake of you

From this day forward I vow this truth

Every day I promise to love myself first

To remind myself of the brilliance of my inner
   beauty

To remind myself that the opinions of you only hold
   as much weight as I allow them

From this moment forward

I will do all it takes

To remain true to me!

— Kenajawa LaShawn

"

I Will Not Tolerate Disrespect

"

As women, we have a lot to deal with on a continuous basis. We have families, careers, friends, and everything in between. Sometimes, the lines can get blurred, and people can step out of character, but one thing we cannot do is tolerate disrespect.

With all the hats that we wear and how tired these may cause us to be, at times, we let the little things slide. Those little things can turn into mountains if they aren't addressed properly. That child that always has a comeback when you say something, or those little ones who roll their eyes as a silent retort… the coworker that always talks over you or the boss who doesn't want your opinion at all… These are just the tip of the iceberg. What we have to do is respectfully let our voices be heard. We have to make sure we are respected without making a scene or causing a commotion.

To show that you will not tolerate disrespect, be sure you are a respectful woman. Don't give people a reason to be disrespectful to you.

— Chantell Williams

"

I Will Not Settle for Less Than
What I Ultimately Deserve

"

We dream of our lives as young girls… the careers we will have… the type of home we will live in… We even know the cars we want, and most importantly, what type of man we will marry. by the time we become adults, we practically have our wedding day planned and are just waiting for that *right* someone to ask for our hand.

Finally, we grow up. We find out that some of those things we wanted and how we wanted them may not be realistic, but...

...we are still hopeful.

Life goes on, and we build happiness in our family, our friends, and our stability. *Did we settle?* of course not! We grew up, and in growing up, we found peace. It's the type of peace that our ten- and twelve-year-old selves couldn't imagine or appreciate, but we still have so much more living to do and so much more to add to our dream!

Settling is not an option once you realize you can always do more—if you choose to: Go back to school. Start that business. Take that position! You can be and do, whatever you put your mind to, so let's go! You can do it!

— Chantell Williams

August

" I Am in Touch with MYSELF "

Sometimes, it is hard to be in tune with ourselves and our needs, especially as women. We are nurturers by nature. Even if we have no kids, we naturally want to care for others. We take the time to learn what others like, what others don't like, what makes others feel loved, and the list could go on. If someone took the time to ask those same questions about us, they would be hard for us to answer. That's because we are not always in touch with ourselves.

After my last break up, I decided I wanted to use all the new free time I had to learn myself. I knew that a lot of the heartaches that I was feeling in life stemmed from the fact that I did not know myself. for example, when someone asked, "Where would you like to eat?"

my immediate response would be, "Where would you like to go? I'll eat what you want." This happened even if I knew what I wanted. My life was so consumed with pleasing others that I did not know Kenajawa at all. After taking the vow to learn myself, I was able to discover myself and get in touch with what it means to love myself.

— Kenajawa LaShawn

August 13

I Will Learn to Love Myself

Learning to love your self is essentially learning to love others. Learning to forgive yourself teaches you how to forgive others. Providing grace to yourself will allow you to give grace to others. How you treat yourself will give you a hint on how you treat others.

There are 3 reasons self-love is important.

* You attract how you feel. When you feel love or positivity, you will attract lovely positive people!
* Secondly, self-love leads to healthier relationships with others. When you are confident in yourself and who you are, you are more open to be happy for the personal accomplishments of your friends even before you reach your highest self-actualization.
* And lastly, when it comes to romantic relationships two halves don't make a whole. Two wholes create wholeness! A lot of relationship

issues come from personal insecurities. This can lead to trust issues, disrespect and loneliness.

★ Write down 1 affirmation for the next 30 days that relates to self-love.

— Cortney D. Surrency, AC-CHC

14

August

Black Berry OR Pina Colada... Whatever I Am, I LOVE My Style Boo!

We live in a world where being an "influencer" has become a lucrative career. There are more followers than leaders, and originality has become rare. to this, I say,

Embrace Your Uniqueness!

Love yourself, flaws and all! Take that which makes you most self-conscious and make it your best feature.

Flaunt it, Girl!

Take time and learn who you are. Then, flow with what feels right... what feels good to you. Your style includes the circle of people you surround yourself with, your living space, the clothes you wear, even where and how you choose to make a living. Make a statement when you walk into a room because your style is also how you carry yourself: head up and shoulders back.

Always remember you were made in His image. Your perfections and imperfections—dress 'em up and wear it *proudly*. Do this if for no other reason than to *not* look foolish trying to be someone you're not. Be YOU, and while you're doing that, work on becoming a BETTER version of YOURSELF. Love your style! You never know who you're inspiring to love themselves and accept who they truly are.

— Monique Carter

"

I Don't Need Makeup

"

I recall dating this guy... he made it mandatory that I dress up all the time and put on makeup all the time. At first, I didn't mind—I liked a man who looked nice too. Eventually, it became demeaning. If I didn't wear makeup or dress a certain way, he left me feeling less than—as if I was not good enough because I did not live up to his expectations. Even after it was over, I still wore makeup each day and never left the house looking anything less than my best. Then, one day, I had to be honest with myself. I told myself that I didn't need makeup—my beauty was not defined by what was on my face, how my face looked, or the things that I wore. Beauty is more than that. Beauty is who I am.

After this, I began refining the woman that I am, and this is when my beauty became radiant. Now, the next time that one comes around, he won't be able to define my beauty because my beauty is defined by My Father.

If you are reading this, and your struggle was or is similar to mine, it's time to redefine your concept of beauty.

We also must stop allowing the world to define what our beauty is.

If you need to hear it... take it from me:

No!

You don't need makeup!

— Kenajawa LaShawn

Say Aloud: **I Don't Need Makeup**

I Am Confident!

Recently, someone told me that I have ego issues, and I got offended. Why? Because they didn't understand the fact that, today, I am able to walk with confidence because I have finally found my worth. They weren't there the days I cried in the mirror because everyone thought I was too skinny, and people constantly reminded me that I needed to gain weight. They didn't know that my peers would ridicule me because I didn't have the nicest clothes or shoes or when people didn't understand the scope of my learning disabilities. How about when my curly, kinky hair wasn't acceptable because it was not long enough to past my shoulders or when I went through the phase of hating myself because guys didn't show me attention...

I wanted to scream:

"I AM NOT CONCEITED! I AM CONFIDENT!"

Today, I am able to walk with my head higher because I have taken the power from people to define my life. I realize that my confidence comes from God. He has already called me accepted, worthy, valuable, and loved. He says the same about you! Read 1 Peter 2:9 anytime you need a reminder of why you can be confident!

— Kenajawa LaShawn

Say Aloud: **I Am Confident!**

I Love EVERY Fiber of My Being

At times, I find that I can be my own worst enemy. While the rest of the world can be so tough, and sometimes even cruel, no one is tougher on me than I am. I'm always wanting and expecting more; nothing is ever good enough. I give myself no pats on the backs or, "Good job!" encourage. I just burden myself with thoughts of what I could have done better. While it may occasionally be good to challenge oneself or to seek improvement, all too often, we get so caught up in where we want to be that we forget to acknowledge and be grateful for where we have been and where we are now.

With every flaw that I have, I need to know that I am an amazing person who has overcome so much while still maintaining a caring heart. That is enough to be proud of, so when I look in the mirror and feel down because all I can focus on are flaws, I remind myself that those flaws come from obstacles I have overcome. From my mind and spirit and everything in between, I have learned to love every fiber of my being, and this is by far the best and most complete love I have ever experienced.

— Brittany Whigham

Say Aloud: **I Love EVERY Fiber of My Being**

August 18

18

I Will Protect My Identity

For too long, I allowed people to take from me. I did not know who I was. in 2015, I learned that I was a part of a royal family, and we all know that the royal family doesn't get treated just any type of way. Once my Father told me who I was, I had to stop just giving anyone access to royalty.

At one time, I found myself questioning why people didn't genuinely love me. My family was distant, friendships didn't last long, and I just felt used in relationships. I didn't know who I was, so I didn't know how I should be loved. God changed that for me. He confirmed my identity and therefore confirmed how I should be treated. I Peter 2:9 became one of my favorite scriptures of confirmation in my identity. This scripture tells me that I am not like others; I am chosen. Scripture calls me royalty. Scripture calls me holy. Scripture tells me that I am God's child. Through my identity, I am able to help others. by calling me out of darkness and into light, God confirmed the identity that was established for me. I can now walk differently. I talk differently, and I act differently— not because I now know who I am but because I know whose I am!

Do you?

— Kenajawa LaShawn

Affirmation Journal

- ★ What does my identity consist of?
- ★ What defines me?
- ★ How can I honor this identity?
- ★ What must I do to protect it?
- ★ How can I make sure others do the same?

"
I Will Leave the Past Behind
"

My past is just that: it's a thing of the past. It's something I have moved through and from, but I will not let the trials and tribulations of my past continue to weigh so heavily on the spirit of the person I am today.

Whether the "miss-takes" be actions that I took myself that led me to fall off track or if they are the actions of others that I allowed in my life who meant me no good, I will release all feelings of anger, sadness, sorrow, and pity. While those experiences from my past may have shaped my growth, those thoughts and feelings have no power over the person I have become. They cannot hold me back unless I allow it. I

will take the momentum that the pain has provided and use it to continually take my life to heights I never dreamed I could attain. I will not be stagnant. I will keep moving, pushing, striving for growth, and

improvement because I have not yet reached my final form. I am still morphing and transforming from the same things that were meant to break me, but I will not allow my past to hold me back from the possibilities of my future.

— Brittany Whigham

Say Aloud: **I Will Leave the Past Behind**

August

My Past is a Stepping Stone to My Destiny

The past sometimes comes back to haunt us; it's not always easy to move forward, but once we've repented and asked God for forgiveness, we are no longer that person. the devil will always bring up your past, or send friendly reminders, but you must realize that you've been given a new beginning.

The only time it should matter what you used to be is when you're ministering to someone about the great things God can do. Your past can be used to bring future souls into the kingdom because it was not so long ago that you were just like them, but know this: stop allowing the past to stop you and use it as a stepping stone to your destiny.

— LoLo Stoney

This Woman's Work (Today)

* List the parts of your past that try to haunt you.
* Beneath that, write, "I AM FORGIVEN!"
* Beneath that, write, "I FORGIVE MYSELF!"
* Take your list, ball it up, and throw it away.
* Repeat as needed to move past your past!

"

I Will KEEP on Keeping On!

"

Life happens every day, and while one day can be a great day, the next day can be the worst. Whether your days be good or bad, continue to push forward with a positive spirit. Times may get tough, and times may be trying, but in this life, the only way out is through. Don't let one bad day ruin what could be a pretty good week.

There is no way around bad days. Although being outwardly good doesn't guarantee sunny skies and rainbows, remain confidently optimistic. in those moments, when being "good" doesn't seem to be as rewarding as it could be, keep pushing and moving forward with a positive mindset. Don't let a minor setback drag down the positivity you are trying to manifest into your life. Don't let negative outside influences sway you.

Attitude is everything, and your attitude should be the determining factor in your life experiences. Keep pushing for greatness. Keep being positive. Keep having a positive attitude. Keep growing. Keep getting better. Keep moving to the beat of your own drum. Whatever you do in this life, just keep on going! Keep on KEEPING on!

— Brittany Whigham

Say Aloud: **I Will KEEP on Keeping On!**

August 22

I Learn from My Mistakes

"I am sorry."

"I apologize."

"I will do better."

These are all phrases we should have in our vocabulary. A person who is unwilling to change or learn from past mistakes is a person who will end up alone. Every day you walk this earth, you will make a mistake--knowingly or unknowingly. the times when you know that you have messed up are the ones that matter the most because these are moments that teach us. Learning from your mistakes brings about growth and ultimately changes the way you navigate through life. These learnings also make you relatable and more approachable.

To the woman who thinks she can do no wrong, you have already failed yourself. Never be above a teaching or learning moment, and never forget to be gracious. No one wants to be taken for granted.

— Chantell Williams

August 23

Mistakes Happen, and Mistakes Are OK!

Mistakes are inevitable. Actually, mistakes are necessary for success. When referring to mistakes, we think of them as failures. I like to think of mistakes as taking calculated chances. When making mistakes, one tries to move on quickly from them. Denial, blame, and excuses usually follow. These happen right before a person thinks to give up.

There are four alternative responses to making a mistake.

★ **First, feel and reflect.**

Take time to process how you feel and reflect on your processes like what went well and what you can do differently.

★ **Secondly, accept appropriate responsibility.**

We often focus on the things that we couldn't control instead of learning from what we actually had a role in. Taking on too much responsibility could add on a lot of pressure that you may not be ready for. When dividing roles and responsibilities, give tasks that complement the natural strengths of an individual.

★ **Next, you should admit and reframe.**

Own up to your misstep and refrain from dwelling on the mistake. This will allow creative energy to flow and see another route to success in the process of reframing.

★ **Lastly, take action!**

Now that you've had time to process your feelings, reflect on the misstep, and develop a new plan, confidently activate your plan and rework it as needed.

Remember you may make a million different mistakes, but the key is never to make the same mistake twice. Its learning from your mistakes that will get you closer to success!

— Cortney D. Surrency, AC-CHC

It's Never a Failure. It's Always a Lesson.

It's never a failure when you've loved
It's never a failure when you tried your best
It's never a failure when you have fought your
*   best fight*
It's never a failure when you persevered
It's never a failure when you've trusted
It's never a failure when you've given
It's never failure when you've cried
It's never a failure when you've Let it Go

The righteous fall seven times
but still get up.

Proverbs 24:16

— Kelly Gardner

It's Okay Not to Have Life Figured Out!

At age 20, I felt like I was so behind in life because it seemed like everyone around me had it all together. All my friends had cars. They were preparing for graduation and starting jobs that paid more than minimum wage. Everyone on social media seemed to be in a thriving, loving relationship. Peers were taking exotic trips to places I couldn't even pronounce...

WHAT WAS WRONG with ME?

By age 22, I figured out that most people were just pretending to have it all together. It is so easy to live behind a mask or for us to live behind the veil of social media. But... that's all so exhausting! I did it for a while too. I would fake to have money to keep up with friends. I smiled like everything was okay when inside, I was really miserable.

Freedom came when I realized I did not have to have life all figured out. Life is a progression. We will always continue to grow, learn, and develop, so as we progress to each stage of life, there will be something new to figure out.

Today, I may not have it all together, but today will teach me a lesson that I can use tomorrow, and that's all I need to keep progressing in this thing called life!

— Kenajawa LaShawn

August

"

Girl! You Got This!

"

Everything you need to be who you are is already on the inside of you. You started off as a seed planted in your mother's womb, and at that very moment, everything that you needed to be who you are destined to be was already on the inside of you!

Often, we go through life seeking our purpose, seeking things to connect to, searching for what we are destined to become without realizing that everything we need is already inside us. You never see anyone putting a tree inside of a seed because, as small as the seed is, the tree resides within it. with proper fertilization and a good environment, the tree grows from the seed.

You don't have to search on the outside to discover who you are and what you can be; you just have to look within. Look within your soul. Look within your heart, your mind, and your body. Who you are is already within you, you just have to tap in to your inner superpower and believe that you are already equipped to do everything you were put here on this earth to do. Take time to dive into your innermost parts and discover your inner beauty. Discover your inner superpower because that's what makes you who you are. Know that you can accomplish many great things because you've already got just what it takes. You've GOT this!

— Coach Mechelle Canady

August 27

I Will Invest in Myself

I will invest in myself. I will pour into myself. I will encourage myself. I will lift myself up. I will prepare myself for this next season. I will go after it ALL. I will speak life into myself.

I will encourage ME to push myself even when I don't want to go any further. I will invest in ME.

I will plant positivity in every area of my life. I will plant determination. I will plant boldness. I will plant wisdom. I will plant love. I will plant peace. I will plant joy. I will make sure that I have prepared myself for whatever God has chosen for me to do.

— Coach Latoya Kight

Affirmation Journal

★ How do I invest in myself?
★ How am I preparing myself for my future?
★ How do I keep myself encouraged to go further?
★ What areas of my life need more positivity?
★ What am I doing about that?

"

I Can Never Have Enough Handbags

"

As I walk, it hangs at my side, making sure all my business remains a secret. It has multiple compartments, and some even have matching accessories. I can choose any size—small, medium, or large—and they come in any color I can imagine. I put it in the seat next to me each time I get in the car, and I always remember never to put it on the floor. It is one of the best gifts a woman can get for any occasion, and it is guaranteed to be used more than once. When it's time for a girls' night out, I remove the strap and put it carefully under my arm, making sure it gets no stains or scuffs. After a while, it's time for a new one. I want the brown one... maybe even the black one... you know... those multipurpose colors...

I can never be too sure, so I'll get them both!

You know...

...a girl can never have too many handbags!

— Chantell Williams

"

I Will Evolve into a Better Version of ME

"

Being a better *you* is not just about reading, writing, and speaking well. Your betterment dives deep into your spirit, soul, and body. Betterment includes allowing yourself to evolve mentally. It's about taking your power back and discovering who you were born to be in life. Betterment is about choosing to believe in YOU—no matter what's happening around you. Through cultivating and planting seeds within, you foster good ground internally and externally.

In pushing yourself toward betterment, you press past familiar limits and step into a realm of uncertainty.

Think about what a better you would look like and challenge yourself to PUSH. Push yourself with intent. Affirm who you are and push toward a better version of you. Don't just learn a new language, read another book, or take another course without evaluating how these things will help you push past who you currently are. Push with *purpose* and change with excitement. Grow in grace and fight fear without flight.

Make a creed today to continually push yourself to evolve into a better version of you.

— Regina N Roberts

August

" I Will STAY in the Process "

Research has shown that it takes a palm tree four to six years to grow to its maximum height of around 30 feet. When a palm tree is planted, no growth is seen for the first two to three years. Even though you can't see it happening, the palm tree is growing. You see no growth above grown, yet the palm tree is growing roots, so when the storm comes, it is able to withstand the wind and the rain. to the naked eye, it really appears that nothing is happening, but the trained observer knows that the palm tree is in the growth process. the seed has been planted, but when you can't see any growth from the tree, the seed just appears to be buried instead.

The process of planting and the process of being buried both look the same, but the difference is in the result.

I want to encourage you now. Even though you may feel buried, stay in the process. Don't interrupt the process. You may feel underground right now, but I encourage you to know and understand that even though you may not see any growth, and you may not feel that you're making progress, stay in the process. Trust it. Don't allow yourself to offset the process because if you stay in the process, in due time, you'll have deep roots that will sustain you if a storm hits. This undercover development time is the time where you grow stronger; this is the time where you grow bigger. Don't give up! Keep growing even when you see no growth and stay in the process no matter what it looks like.

— Coach Mechelle Canady

August

I LOVE ME!

As children, we are taught how to love others, yet we are not often taught how to love ourselves. Even though scripture says to love our neighbors as ourselves, grammatically, the latter part has to come before the first part. You have to love yourself before you can love others. Ultimately, we struggle with how to love others because we don't know how to love ourselves. We must learn to love ourselves and fall deeply in love with who we are while also embracing who we are not. We must love ourselves unconditionally the same way we try to love others unconditionally. We must love ourselves and be kind to ourselves, just as we are kind to others. by not being over-critical and by not being our biggest critic, we practice loving ourselves through understanding just who we are.

Get to know who you are and take time to be with *you*. I challenge you today to take some time to review the ways you are able to love you better so that you can better love others. in this season, don't just love yourself, but work to fall in love with yourself! Spend time with yourself. Show that you care about yourself. Work on yourself, and the more you begin to love on yourself, the easier you will find it to love others too.

— Coach Mechelle Canady

Grace & Mercy!

September

I Am A Lady of Grace

Grace is most often described as God's unmerited favor because it is. Grace from God is very evident in our lives when we need it most but deserve it least. Being a lady of grace requires an honest perspective about shortcomings, sin, habits, faults, failures, and the many issues we have to contend with. It is when we can look beyond the adornments and accoutrements: bank accounts, cars, houses, accomplishments, awards, acquaintances, and accolades. in seeing the depths of where we could be, have been, or who we really are—versus who people think we are—we gain an understanding of grace that makes it all the more amazing. We receive it daily when we awaken. We fall asleep and rest in it every night, whether we have an awareness of it or not, so we receive it and extend it to others.

A lady of grace sees herself through the eyes of faith and the covering of mercy. Fully embracing grace means extending, to ourselves and others, the opportunity to transform and be renewed without the weight of condemnation. Grace requires a heart of gratitude that makes space for growth and change. Mistakes and misgivings provide wisdom and life lessons for a better way and a brighter future. the journey of life is an unpredictable one for sure. Grace gives us the ability to freely do and to freely live... to be in the fullness of who we are intended to be... one day, hour, minute, and one moment at a time.

No matter what, a lady of grace counts her blessings. She makes her way through life with confident authority and assurance of who she belongs to. Though she sometimes gets what she doesn't deserve, she stands tall and carries the fragrance of God's glory with a grateful heart.

— Dr. Latisha D. Reeves Henry

September 2

I Will Work on Gentleness

I am soft to the touch. I am tender. I am mild-mannered and kind. What am I?

I am gentleness.

I don't know if we truly know the meaning of the word or even if we have the ability to *be* it. We have been taught to be strong and to not let people walk over us, so gentleness is reserved only for those we love.

We have been told to never show our weaknesses, so people could never have the upper hand on us, but is that really beneficial? Can we just turn it on and turn it off like that? Is there a happy medium that some of us have forgotten about? We seem to have more patience to be more gentle toward those we know versus those we don't know. We have a low tolerance for people and things that irritate us, and we don't have a problem showing it. So, with that being said, I have a challenge for you:

The next bad moment that you have, whether it be today or in the days to come, sow a positive seed and walk away. Remember that in some cases, your silence can speak much louder than your words ever could.

— Chantell Williams

This Woman's Work (This Week)

- ★ List 10 examples or traits of gentleness.
- ★ List 5 people you need to be gentler with.
- ★ Take time this week to hand write letters to each of these people.
- ★ Include a few of the things from your list on gentleness.
- ★ *Don't forget to mail your letters!!!*

September 3

I Am Slow to Speak

*"This, you know, my beloved brethren. But everyone must be
quick to hear, slow to speak, and slow to anger."*

James 1:19 NASB

I have learned,

and I am still learning to be cautious about what I say.

No longer do I follow the belief that,

"I say what I want when I want."

I am working on using a filter on what I say

and the way I say it.

I now think about

how it will affect the person I'm talking to.

I realized I must care about the feelings of others

more than I care about the need to speak my mind

recklessly.

Ego says not to care.

Flesh says they will be okay.

Wisdom says, be careful.

God says, watch your mouth.

My growth depends

on me changing my usual and operating differently.

— Coach Latoya Kight

Affirmation Journal

★ Where in life am I being reckless with my words?

★ What impact does this have on others?

★ What is God saying to me about this challenge?

★ How can I be slowing to speak?

★ What will I gain in the end?

September 4

I Am Slow to Anger

You ever noticed how manageable a situation becomes when we don't immediately react in anger and rage? Consider that one time in traffic when you let anger take over or that last argument when you just had to have the last word. What about the time you were angrily looking for something? As soon as you calmed down, you found it.

Allowing someone or something to make us angry strips us of our power. in turn, we give them power over us.

Being slow to anger shows self-control, tremendous strength, and it allows you to keep a clear mind for thinking strategically versus erratically. Being quick-tempered has landed many otherwise decent people behind bars filled with regret, wishing they'd made a different decision. Let's also keep in mind how anger leads to stress, which can lead to health issues and concerns. This includes high blood pressure, ulcers, and headaches. You don't want these problems!

To control yourself in undesirable situations in the future, practice deep breathing and listen to understand rather than to respond. Finally, know that most anger projected upon you has nothing to do with you. It is more based on personal and internal issues the other person is experiencing in their lives, so learn not to take things too personally, and you'll be alright!

— Monique Carter

Say Aloud: **I Am Slow to Anger**

September 5

" I Am a Woman of Peace and Not War "

I protect my space. I protect my mind. I protect my heart. Anything that's trying to infect those areas MUST go! I refuse to interrupt my peace for the sake of anyone or any place. I HATE conflict! I HATE intense situations! If I can avoid arguments, I will with all my might. I bring peace, so I expect peace. I respect people, so I expect it in return. I practice conflict resolution so I can calmly resolve an issue. I aim for peace and avoid war at all costs.

Nothing good comes from war when you're in it for self-gratification. You will only produce death and negativity in the end.

Being peaceful is always my goal. When I'm faced with a crazy situation, my thoughts are on the best way to get out of it without causing harm to myself or anyone else. I continually work to be an all-around peaceful person because I am a woman of peace and not war.

—— Coach Latoya Kight

September 6

" I Will Bring Joy to Lives of Others "

I will bring joy to the lives of others!
The decision to celebrate and appreciate
others brings me joy.
Being able to express a level of hope, love,
and grace to others provides joy.

The state of joy should always be present as you grow through life.

I will bring joy to others by sharing my story and my triumphs of good and bad.
I will bring joy to the lives of others through words of encouragement.

— Regina N Roberts

September

I Give to Others

Giving is better than receiving. That's so true! There really is a health benefit when we give to others. Giving can reduce stress and lower your blood pressure. There is also a spiritual benefit giving to others. When the spirit leads you to give, you are sowing a harvest!

We should look at giving as a duty and not only as an act of kindness, so I would encourage you to give when you feel lead. to ensure that you are doing what is asked of you by God, you must always have your listening ears on. We sometimes casually give and then feel some type of way when the receiver doesn't do with—or receive—the gift the way we wanted them to. Consulting with the Holy Spirit first can help you give more confidently. It will be very clear to you when you gave in the spirit. You will feel good by the act and not be moved by the way your gift was received. There is also supernatural element when you give in the spirit. You will find that the gift is exactly what the receiver needed! So, start getting healthy and start giving because your life depends on it!

— Cortney D. Surrency, AC-CHC

September

I Am Forgiving

One of the most challenging things to do is to forgive those who have wronged, embarrassed, ashamed or wounded us deeply. It can be hard to forgive because it goes against how we feel, what we think, and what we want or deserve. When we are wronged, our feelings lead us to rehearse the episode of the offense and how it made us feel. We replay it repeatedly like a highlight reel. the increasing feeling of offense governs our thoughts. We think, "It is not fair," or "I will not take this." "I am done!" we say, or we choose to be passive-aggressive, and we call it by the cuter name: petty. Then, there are more serious offenses that hinder or rob us of our ability to receive the fullness of God's forgiving grace.

Matthew 6:14-15 reveals to us that we must extend forgiveness in order to be fully forgiven by the Father. Christ told the parable of the man who was forgiven of much but was thrown into prison to pay His debt because He refused to forgive the debt of another. We see that unforgiveness blocks the blessing of our being completely released to receive all the grace God extends to walk in our giftings and to breathe in life, fully. Forgiveness is a choice we make not to follow our feelings, thoughts, or desires, but to obey the command to extend what we have received while letting God be in charge of the rest.

I forgive because I am forgiven.

— Dr. Latisha D. Reeves Henry

This Woman's Work (This Month)

★ *List names of 5 people you need to forgive.*
★ *Live 5 people who need to forgive you.*
★ *Take time this month to call these people and get it off your chest... FORGIVE THEM!*

September

9

"

I Will Let It Go

"

Women are nurturers to the core. Because of that, we often ignore challenges and opportunities that are right before us... like the feeling you get when you know you can do better, but you just can't move! Something in you won't let you walk away from *it*. You hope things are going to be different each time, but what if *it* doesn't change? What if *it* gets worse? Are you willing to sacrifice your peace or joy to have *it*?

Take a moment to self-reflect on what *it* is that you may have, or may need to, let go of. Once you have it in your mind, consider how the thought of *it* makes you feel. Is *it* something you can take pride in having, or is *it* something that you would rather not share?

NOW is the time to set some things in motion and finally **let *it* go!**

— Chantell Williams

September

10

"

It is Okay to Let Go

"

It's okay to let go. Sometimes you love someone who just does not love you back. Because of this, you should let them go.

The life you are living is a journey, and on this journey, you should experience, not just giving love, but being loved as well.

Love is a wonderful and beautiful thing. When you love someone, you desire to see that person happy and fulfilled, in good health, and full of great cheer. When you love someone, you are doing those things that will contribute to that person being just that happy and fulfilled, in good health, and full of great cheer.

Sometimes, feelings and actions are not reciprocated. When you find yourself in those times, it may be best to let go. If you decide to do so, understand that you are not just letting go so you can find another person to reciprocate your feelings and actions; you are letting go so that the person you love can find the person they love. You let go so your love can be free to find the person who can share desires and express actions of love. You let go so you can be free to give and to receive love.

— Kwanza Yates

September 11

"

I Am FREE!

"

I AM FREE! the crazy part of this statement is that before, I didn't even know I was in bondage. When trying to explain to others the freedom that is experienced in Christ, it's always hard to articulate.

Below, I list a few ways I have experienced freedom in Christ:

★ **Freedom from Heartbreak** – I learned, after finding my relationship with God, that a lot of the heartache I experienced was self-inflicted. Why? Because I didn't listen when the signs said, "No!" I didn't listen when the person said, "No!" I didn't even listen when I would say, "No!" Being free has helped me to listen to the warnings. I have now gained confidence in understanding why the wait is worth it—*it's for the sake of my sanity! lol*

★ **Freedom from Insecurities** – Simply put, once I learned whose I am, then I understood **Who I Am!** God gives me the freedom to be myself—to not be restrained by the things that the world says I should be insecure about. God gives me security!

★ **Freedom from Toxic Relationships** – Whew! Being a people pleaser, I always found myself holding on to relationships for too long. Not all toxic relationships seem bad, but in all types of relationships, I believe that both individuals involved should be a benefit to each other. So, I realized I just needed to distance myself a little from some friendships because I was being drained. *Evaluate the relationships in your life, and make sure that you are not losing yourself trying to keep the relationship.*

★ **Freedom to Live Out My Dreams** – Psalm 37:4 says, "Delight yourself in the Lord, and He will give you the desires of your heart." Sometimes, society can make it seem like such a hassle to accomplish your dreams. Once I devoted myself to God, I saw him open doors to me that neither I nor anyone else could explain. I realized that my Father wants to see me accomplish all my dreams. As long as I continue to trust Him with them with my dreams, they *will* come true!

★ **Freedom to Help Others Find Freedom** – There is freedom in helping others find their freedom too. I know that the promises my Father has for me are not only for me; they are for all of us, so I want to live out my purpose and help others find their freedom as well!

— Kenajawa LaShawn

September

My Strength Keeps Me Grounded.
My Strength Sets Me FREE!

Being strong is different from having strength. I believe that, at times, we confuse the two. As women, we take on the responsibility of being *strong* for others rather than encountering and embracing our strength. Strength is that which allows us to be vulnerable without weakness. Strength is that which allows us to not only be GREAT at the 9-5, but we still handle responsibilities outside of work, and we do it with an essence of grace as no man can.

You are made in God's image to be the authentic you in and out. God gave you a strength that you can't deny. It doesn't even matter how you got here, or the circumstances of your life. God has you here for a purpose. Whether that purpose is to encourage, love his people, *or get annoyed by them*—children included— He gave you a gender that will RISE to the occasion. Your strength will be measured by your actions, your ability, your truth... and the WORLD will be better because of the strength and power that you possess.

Amen and Ashe.

We call the ancestors into our presence.

— Stephanie Hamilton Muwunganirwa

Affirmation Journal
★   What does it mean to be created in God's image?
★   How have I experienced God's strength and power?
★   How has that strength kept me grounded?

September

As I Heal Myself,
I Will Help Heal the Women Around Me

I have learned that life is all about experiences. Most of our memories are associated with something we felt in that moment—in the experience. Whether you know it or not, you are experiencing something today—good or bad—that will help someone tomorrow.

For the majority of my life, I had not experienced what it feels like for someone close to me to pass away. When someone I knew experienced the loss of someone they loved, I always felt awkward because I did not know how to identify with that feeling. People around me did pass, but death did not affect me like I saw it affect others.

My first time experiencing the loss of someone close to me was the loss of my son, who was stillborn at 8 ½ months. At the time, I was 20 years old. I had just begun my relationship with God and had accepted the fact that I could be a good mom, so this was a hard time for me. Going through this trial allowed me to now share a special bond with other women who have experienced the loss of their child. Daily, God is showing me how my testimony will be used for the healing of other women. I know that this will be a continual process of healing for me, but as I am learning to heal and cope, I will be able to help other women around me do the same.

There are things that we are experiencing in life that can help us to help someone else. One of my favorite scriptures is Genesis

50:20. It states, "You intended to harm me, but God intended it all for good. He brought me to this position so I could save the lives of many people." This scripture tells me that all the things I have endured will help save someone else's life.

What are you going through today that can help someone else tomorrow?

— Kenajawa LaShawn

September 14

I Am A Vessel

It seems the bad news always outweighs the good news. Headlines read, "Multiple dead in a mass shooting," "Homelessness is increasing," "Affordable healthcare is decreasing," "Terrorist attacks imminent," "Child missing," "The economy is dwindling..." All around us, we can easily find reasons to be fearful and hopeless, but we must remember that although these things may be taking place around us, they do not have to be taking place within us.

By being a vessel, we secure something on the inside that is separate and protected from the outside. Therefore, when the world around us shows us the reasons why we should be afraid and angry, we can be equipped to respond with braveness and compassion. When the world around us shows us the reasons why we should be hateful, we can respond with love. When the world around us shows us the reasons why we should be indifferent, we can respond with compassion.

By being a vessel, we decide what goodness we will hold on the inside and project to the world around us. This is the first step in changing the bad news into good news.

Be a vessel. Change the headline.

— Kwanza Yates

September

I Am Patient with Myself and Those Around Me

I am Patient with..........
Myself
My Children
My Spouse
My Co-Workers
My Boss
My Friends
My Acquaintance
My Tribulations

Let your hope keep you joyful

> **Rejoice in your hope,**
> **be patient in trouble,**
> **and keep on praying.**

Romans 12:12

— *Kelly Gardner*

Affirmation Journal
* *How do I demonstrate my patience?*
* *How can I better demonstrate patience?*
* *What are the benefits of my patience?*

I Will Say What Needs to Be Said

We have one life to live, and no... we aren't always happy with it, but it's the one God gave us, so I'm inclined to ask: How can we look at some other woman's flaws and decide that her flaws are all that she is? Women are so much more than attitudes, negativity, and difficult dispositions, but because we pass judgment on our sisters so quickly, we never get to see the real woman on the inside. We all play the blame game, but when was the last time you did a self-assessment and really worked on you? When was the last time you said—to yourself—the things that needed to be said?

Pray this prayer with me:

God, give me the strength I need to survive and the will to press on despite my faults. I won't always get it right, yet I won't let the things that I didn't do right hold me down. I will extend grace to women because *we* deserve it. I will show mercy and keep pushing. I will speak life into my sisters and guide her as she grows through saying to her the things that only another woman can. Amen.

People can say what they want, but words do hurt. Words can kill a woman's growth or cause her to stumble. When you are sharing with your sisters the things that need to be said, be clear, but don't be ugly and don't be unreasonable.

— Chantell Williams

This Woman's Work (This Week)

★ List 5 things that you have *not* said that should be said.
★ List 5 people who you need to have major convos with.
★ Consider what happens if you don't say/do these things.
★ Consider what happens if you do say/do these things.
★ for each item, decide if you will move forward or not.

September

There's No Promotion Without Pressure

Many years ago, I read a quote that said, "The darkest hour comes right before the dawn." When we are in our darkest hour and can't see your way out, we have to trust and believe that when the night ends, morning comes. the Bible says, in Psalms 30:7, "...weeping may endure for a night, but joy comes in the morning." You may be under lots of pressure right now, but that pressure is making you into something great. Just know that no promotion comes without pressure.

Right before good things in your life start to take place, you might find yourself in a place of chaos. Diamonds are developed from a lump of coal that is best when it is burned to ashes and is no longer worth anything. If the right amount of pressure is applied to that same lump of coal, it becomes a diamond.

Right now, you may be a diamond in the rough, but stand through the pressure because there is a diamond in you. Don't be discouraged because it's dark right now. Know that the pressure is going to produce the promotion. Don't give up thinking life is at its worst because the darkest hour of the night comes just before the day. Stay in the pressures of life; there is a diamond waiting to come forth.

— Coach Mechelle Canady

257

Page

"If I Don't Deal with It, It Will Deal with Me.

Do you find yourself holding things in?

It was hard to admit that I had a problem... for a long time, I saw avoiding conflict as a good thing. I would keep all my emotions and feelings to myself. No matter how hurt I was, a smile stayed on my face, and my response was always, "I am okay." for a while, I would be fine, or I would let everything out on my own sometime later.

One day a friend pulled me aside. She asked if she had done something to hurt my feelings. I let her know that everything was fine, and I plastered my secured smile back across my face. She said, "No, it's not. You've been distant from me lately." I had become so normalized to my traits that I didn't even realize I was distancing myself... because of my hurt.

Since that time, I have become more aware of the fact that it is okay to vocalize my emotions and hurts. I have accepted that it is okay to stand up for myself instead of validating someone else's feelings at the expense of tucking my hurt feelings away. I have learned that, in any healthy relationship, you will be able to talk through circumstances and get them resolved.

Because if you don't deal with it, it will most certainly deal with you!

— Kenajawa LaShawn

September 19

I Own My MESS So I Can Be Better

Acknowledging something you have done wrong and owning something you have done wrong are two different things. You may acknowledge or admit that you lied, stole, hurt, endangered, broke trust, turned your back, let down, disappointed, or caused someone pain...

...but until you own it, sit in it for a while, sit with what you have done for a while—to yourself and to others—get angry at it, get angry at yourself, cry, and cry, and then cry some more...

...until you own your MESS, you can't rise out of it. Until you get real with yourself and your God about your mess, you will continue to live in the lie. You will continue to be mediocre, never rising to your potential. You will continue to settle for less than because you don't believe you can be, and should be, more than.

Until you own your life, you are just renting and are subject to be evicted at any given moment by trials, tribulations...

...and haters.

— Kwanza Yates

September 20

I Will Walk Away from Painful Situations

I will walk away from that which causes discomfort and suffering.

Have you ever bought and wore a pair of shoes that you fell in love with the first time you spotted them on the rack? Ever bought a pair of shoes that were a size too big or a size too small? Although you realized the size or FIT wouldn't work, you still purchased the shoe. You contemplated whether you would purchase them or not... the shoe made you a little taller... a side view made you look 10 lbs. slimmer... in the end, you just had to have the shoe because it was your favorite color *(or maybe it made you feel adorned and glamorous!!!).* Let's compare this example to how we endure pain.

As women, we experience pain, and then we wear it longer than we should. We hold on to pain, allowing it to consume us. We endure the pain the same way we continue to wear that favorite shoe. Continually accepting pain and harboring it longer than we should causes lifelong discomfort and suffering. for your freedom, sanity, and your comfort, walk away from painful situations.

Don't force yourself to stay in a state of discomfort or suffering that will only cause discomfort. Walk away from opportunities that will bring about a lifelong trail of suffering. Instead, put on something that fits you better and chose a path that leads toward passion, peace, and prosperity.

— Regina N Roberts

September

" All Friends Aren't Good Friends. "

Be careful. Every friend that you have doesn't always mean you well. Every friend doesn't have your best interest at heart. Every friend is not trustworthy. Every friend is not loyal. Every friend is not dedicated. Every friend is not positive.

You must turn your discernment on when dealing with others outside of yourself. Some people are just in your space to watch you fall. Some people are only in your face and your space to watch the demise of your success. You must be able to decipher who is for you and who is against you.

Realize that although they may be smiling in your face, some friends have a knife in their hand ready to stab you in the back. the best buffer you'll have for this is to trust and lean on God. Let Him be your eyes and your ears. Get to a point where you can be sure about who does and who does not want to see you win so you can remove who you need to remove and keep who you need to keep.

Everybody doesn't have your back, but that doesn't mean that all your friends are bad. It just means that you must be careful about who you consider to be your friend. Friends are good, but all friends are not good friends.

— Coach Latoya Kight

September

Listen. . .
Her Story is Not My Story

Your mother wasn't there.
Her story isn't your story.
You may be in pain
    from a mother who wasn't what you needed,
but this, my dear,
    is only the start...
God has the finish...
You, my heart,
    do not have to continue self-defeating professes.
You are great and worthy, my heart, and are made in
    the image of God.
You have work to do.
You are as amazingly equipped as everyone you see.
    Your eyes tell the story.
    They will be your truth.
If you want a different story,
    it's your time to CHANGE!

— Stephanie Hamilton Muwunganirwa

I Will Be Quick to Listen and Slow to Speak

Your lips are moving, but I stopped listening fifty-six seconds ago. I've already decided what I wanted to say, so whatever you're rambling on about doesn't matter much to me. I have a point I want to make. I've got you now, so I smugly stand, gloating in my head. Meanwhile, I can't understand why there is a disconnect between us. Why don't you understand my point? Why do you think yours is so valid? the conversation is getting heated. You're frustrated. I'm frustrated. You aren't hearing me though. Why won't you listen? Listen.

I'm not listening. I'm going over my grocery list in my head while I wait for your lips to stop moving so I can hurl out my retort. I don't want to forget what I want to say because it's sure to win this argument, but wait... what are we even arguing for? Listen.

Grocery list. You're STILL talking, droning on and on, about to make me forget my game-winning point. I have to "win" this.

Listen. I just need to listen. I have so much that I want to say, so many feelings to express that I forget to consider your words. Just listen.

Please just listen, your eyes plead. So, listen, I'm listening. My lips part to interrupt, but... I don't speak. I just listen.

How often are you ready and waiting with a response before the other party has even finished their sentence? Far too often, we are engaged in conversations and aren't actively listening to understand one another. We are too eager to get our point across that we forget one major part of communication: listening. Fight the urge to immediately form a rebuttal and just listen. Be sure to hear the other party and take their views into account. It doesn't make your point any less valid to stop and listen to theirs.

— Brittany Whigham

September 24

There is POWER in SUBMISSION, so Walk with Grace!

Submission seems to be an ugly word these days. What people don't understand is that submission is the best way to the heart of God and to hear His voice clearly. Submission makes life so much easier. It's not about control; it's about understanding that there is an order in the way things should go. Altering the flow of order can hinder your next step to your greater. We are often so busy trying to assert our authority or prove a point that we miss the amazement of God. God can't move when we limit Him. We don't recognize how much we limit Him by not abandoning our will so we can give finally into His. When we understand that what we have been doing in our power isn't working, we will be more willing to do it God's way. We will be more willing to submit to God's will.

— Coach Latoya Kight

September

I Will Walk in Love

As women, we wear many hats, so it's easy to get tangled in life. We have our amazing highs and experience some interesting lows, but we manage to always keep going.

Some of us have been in bad relationships, and some of us have had the pleasure of having amazing relationships. We have forgiven people who didn't deserve the forgiveness or even care if we forgave them or not. with everything that happens around us, we still manage to have love for something. Whether it be family, friends, our careers, or our significant other, we always pull good love from the deepest parts of our being.

In our head, we sometimes say we won't ever love again, but when the opportunity presents itself, we can't help but love!

No matter the circumstances... no matter what you have encountered or what you believe you cannot do... always remember to walk in love and extend grace to someone you don't believe deserves it because one day... you may need the same love for yourself.

— Chantell Williams

Affirmation Journal

* What does it mean to walk in love?
* Why do I choose to walk in love?
* What are the long-term benefits of walking in love?
* What are the short-term benefits?
* How do others benefit from the love I display?

September

I Am A Peacemaker

Ladies, have you ever had a moment where something happened, and everything in you wanted to snap? I mean, you have an out of body experience as your mind leaves you and plays out everything you want to do. If you say no to this question, you aren't being honest.

The truth is, we all want to live in peace, but there is always something or someone looking to pull us out of our comfort zone. My mother used to tell me, "You don't give people the power to change your mood or alter your behavior." Honey! I would FREELY give away my peace to act up back then, but as I grew older, I had to change. I don't desire conflict, and nowadays, I can allow things to roll off my back that once set me on fire.

A peacemaker is someone who chooses peace when conflict is the easier choice, and that alone speaks volumes. What will you choose today?

— Chantell Williams

Affirmation Journal

★ Am I a peacemaker?
★ Do I choose peace when conflict is the easier choice?
★ How can I be even more peaceful in my life?
★ What prompted my desire to choose a route of peace?
★ How will I continually make this decision daily?
★ What's my reason why?

September 27

" I Am Forgivable "

There are many things that we can find ourselves doing that are less than admirable. Whether we care to admit it or not, those of us who are of the Christian faith, as well as other persuasions of faith, do often categorize the sins, faults, failures, and mistakes of ourselves and others. Our past, or present, bad decisions or mistakes are often placed in the worse category by others who then cause us to bear the weight of low self-esteem and self-condemnation.

Sister... beloved... please know that there is nothing in the past nor present that is so bad that we cannot be forgiven.

1 John 1:9 NKJV reminds us to confess our sins as God is faithful and just to forgives us and cleanse us from all unrighteousness. Romans 8:1 says there is no condemnation to those who are in Jesus who do not walk according to the flesh, but according to the Spirit.

What that means is I AM FORGIVABLE. It means YOU ARE FORGIVABLE! Shame does not have the final word—Grace does. I am forgivable because the amazing grace of Christ's unconditional love looks beyond my faults—past, present, and future—to see, cover and meet me at the point of my need. I am justified by faith, washed, saved, cleansed, and restored in Jesus Christ. Let us stand tall and walk humbly, thankful to be in the beauty of His light with our crowned heads held high.

We are forgiven.

— Dr. Latisha D. Reeves Henry

September 28

I Am Somebody

"For me, graduation meant freedom. It meant that I did it—I did what they said I could not. I remember moments when I would disappoint my family, and they looked at me with eyes that said, "You're going to be just like your mom." I remember times when my dad was drunk, and He would use those same words to slap me in the face. I was determined not to be bitter, but to be better. At that time in my life, my mom didn't paint a pretty picture in my head. My mother was a person that gave up. She did not care about others. She was an addict, she was a heartbreaker, and she was nothing. These were all the things that I was determined *not* to be. Since I was fighting so hard not to be my parents, I never really got to know myself. When I received my diploma, I did not feel I was receiving it for me. I felt that I was receiving it for all the things I was not."

- Excerpt from *Every Tear Was A Silent Prayer by*
Kenajawa Lashawn

They say the college years are the years when you find yourself. I am finding that to be true. Through the trials I endured in college, I came to realize that I am not a product of my past, but rather, I have the power to write a new future for myself.

I AM SOMEBODY!

I am not my past!

— Kenajawa LaShawn

I Forgive Me

For many years, I struggled with forgiving myself. I couldn't believe how I allowed myself to be in such a dark place. All I thought about what how I went from the pulpit to the club, how I had failed as a mother, and disappointed I was remembering how—after 18 years of marriage—I was standing in divorce court. It wasn't until I *deeply* considered those other people I needed to forgive that I came to the realization that I needed to start first by forgiving... myself.

I needed to forgive ME!

We struggle with forgiving others, mostly because we struggle with forgiving ourselves. Once I was able to accept the fact that I had been hurt and acknowledge the fact that I didn't do everything right, I was able to make the necessary adjustments and forgive me.

Forgiveness starts within you. Walking in unforgiveness is like being locked in jail, all while having the keys to your freedom right there in your hand. Don't be a prisoner to unforgiveness. Start by forgiving *you*.

It took some time, but one day, I was finally able to walk to the mirror and look at myself and say, "I forgive you."

That day, I was able to walk away **free**.

— Coach Mechelle Canady

Say Aloud: **I FORGIVE ME! I AM FORGIVEN!**

I Will Walk in Grace

The archaic definition of *walk* is used to describe the way in which someone lives or behaves. How do we consider this definition in relation to someone who is walking in God through grace? We let our past dictate our outlook on life, yet Jesus paid it all for us, so we must honor him and walk like we are new, free from our mistakes, wrongdoings, hurtful thoughts and actions.

Once you have accepted the promise of salvation, you are also free to receive the grace. Nothing in your past should shame you anymore once you accept the fact that the old version of you is dead; you are a new creature in God when you are born again. You are physical, mentally, spiritually, and emotionally reborn. the enemy will try to convince you that you are stilled judged by others and that earthly judgment matters. Don't let the enemy try to convince you that your past will outweigh your new life in Christ. the first step to walking in grace is to own your forgiveness. You have to believe it! Once you believe and receive your forgiveness, you will be able to walk BOLDLY in grace.

— Cortney D. Surrency, AC-CHC

Say Aloud: I Will Walk in Grace

Relate !
& Communicate !

"

I Have A VOICE!
I Use It to Help Others and to Heal My Soul!

"

Learning the power of your own words is the key to living an abundant life. It took some time for me to get here, but learning the strength of my voice provided healing for my soul. Through the years, I have found that my voice that breeds wealth, health, and soothes pain and relaxes anxiety. I have a voice that brings correction. I have a voice that shares a story that forever lives inside me. I have a voice that was once silenced by fear, rejection, and insecurity. Now, I have a voice that is Free, Happy, and Whole.

Learn to appreciate the voice of others, and work to find your own voice by using words of encouragement to help yourself and others every single day. Practice using the power of your words by affirming yourself daily through positive declarations. Use these positive messages to inspire yourself and to support others you come across along the way. Use your voice to declare, to decline, to delight, and to **dream**!!! Use your voice to share your life's testimony with others in ways that will educate, empower, and enrich their lives in return.

I have a voice! You have a voice! WE have a voice!

— Regina N Roberts

Say Aloud: My Voice Helps Others Heal Their Soul!

Affirmation Journal

★ How does my voice help others heal their soul?

★ What types of vocal encouragement and support do I offer others regularly?

★ How can I use my voice as a means of support for those who need it?

October 2

" I Will Be the Change I Want to See "

Wake up each and every day with a renewed sense of—not just purpose—but of being. Be present in each encounter. There may be challenges that come your way, and that is okay! You've got this! You are a woman who possesses the ability to do anything you put your mind to, so go out there and do great things! Now!!! Not later. the world isn't going to make *itself* a better place. If you see a problem, be the solution. No matter how big or small the problem is, all that matters is that *you* put forth some effort for a better tomorrow.

Be kinder in your speech; more generous in charity; more attentive to your family; more understanding as a friend; more productive as an employee; more active in your community. Don't just turn a blind eye to the plight of the world. Be more than a social media commentator to crimes and injustices. Rise to the occasion each day.

We all want to see change, but it requires each of us to be more and to do more.

— Brittany Whigham

Say Aloud: **I Will Be the Change I Want to See!**

October

What I Focus on Will Multiply

The areas that you give the greatest attention to are the areas that will have the greatest gain. That goes for both the positive and the negative areas of life. If you focus on yourself, you will grow. Focus on what makes you who you are!!! Focus on your good, focus on your gifts, and focus on your talents. Focus on what helps you to do WHATEVER it is that you need to do. When you focus on your goals, your dreams, and your aspirations, you will see those things come to pass.

Take a moment and think about where your focus is. Where you are today is based on where your focus was on yesterday; where you will be on tomorrow is based on where your focus is right now. Don't focus on what you don't have. That'll get you nowhere *(AND get you more of the same!)*. Don't get caught up in the cycle of comparison. Focusing on someone else's accomplishments robs the earth of what *you* can become. Place your time, energy, and focus on being the best version of yourself. You will soon see that what you focus on will multiply, so focus on you!

— Coach Mechelle Canady

Affirmation Journal

- ★ What do I spend most of my time focusing on?
- ★ How have I seen these things manifest in my life?
- ★ What should I spend my time focusing on?
- ★ How do I want these things to manifest in my life?

October

My Words Are My Power...

During a poetry event I used to frequent, the host would do a "call and response" at the start of it. He would say, "My words are my power," and the attendees would say, "So let them create." Those words always resonated with me, possibly because they were a weekly reminder of the strength of our words and how they need to be used with care and caution.

Women have the ability to either build up or tear down, and the scars from our words can be carried through generations. Once you have the knowledge of how important your words are, you have to choose them carefully. You need to know your audience and assess whether the words that come out of your mouth are going to help or hinder, and then act accordingly. It is our responsibility to uplift, encourage, and love each other in a way that only women are capable of loving. Our little girls and boys will learn how to reach their potential as adults because of our words and actions. Decide now that the impact you will make on our future leaders will be a positive one. Watch the words that come out of your mouth...

...because my words are my power...

...so, let them create...

...a better future.

— Stephanie Hamilton Muwunganirwa

October

I Will Be Honest with Others

Growing up, we were always told, "If you don't have anything nice to say, don't say anything at all." I can agree with that to a certain degree because sometimes honesty is the only thing that will help in a moment. Imagine your friend asking, "Can you smell my breath?" You say no when the honest response should have been, "Yes, but I have some gum." *haha*

When we deny others of our honest opinion when asked for it, we deny them a growth opportunity. When someone hurts you, it's up to you to tell them how they made you feel. We can't sweep things under the rug and hope they will get better. in the same way, we can expect people to treat us better if we don't tell them how that can happen.

Today, make yourself a promise. From this moment on, be more honest with others in a loving way. This will ensure that you are received in the way that you intended, and if someone just happens to get offended by your polite honesty, apologize to them and try your honesty again on another person the next day. Make a practice of being honest.

— Chantell Williams

This Woman's Work (Today)

- ★ List the people in your life who you have not been honest with.
- ★ Of those, select which ones you need to be honest with.
- ★ Plan time this week to have these conversations.

October

I Will Be Authentic

My definition:
  Authentic – posting a picture...
  ...with no filter.

We are living in an era where filters, make-up, and surgeries are used to easily cover up who we truly are.

DISCLAIMER:
Ladies, there is ABSOLUTELY nothing wrong with fixing yourself up!! But in doing so, you should still... *insert speaker emoji*

BE YOU!

Despite having what some may view as flaws, I urge you to stay true to self. Being authentic is much more than posting a filter-less photo. It is being true to self.

Being Yourself... Being Original... Being 100 *(emoji)*... Being Real... Being any of these requires you to know yourself. If you do not know who you are, begin to study your personality and character traits. Your traits, beliefs, habits, and practices are just some of the things that make up who you are.

★   Do you think your traits, beliefs, habits, and practices effectively portray who you are?

— Erika Harp

Say Aloud: **I Will Be Authentic**

October 7

I Will Be on Time

Punctuality is an area of my life where I could use some improvement. When I am not on time, I am typically about five to ten minutes late. However, I have come to realize that this is unacceptable. I have learned punctuality is imperative because it lets others know that you care. When you are on time, this shows that you are responsible.

I have learned that most people are late because they fail to wake up on time, or they hit snooze one too many times. Oversleeping is not an excuse to be late. It is time to get up and seize the day. There are also those that wake up on time but take their time getting ready, and in turn, become late.

Let's work on this together. I vow to be a more punctual person. Whether this be meeting up with friends or making appointments, every minute of the day is precious and should be treasured. Let's not waste any more time.

—— Arielle Griffin

This Woman's Work (Always)

- ★ To keep from rushing from one thing to the next, leave up to 30 mins of rest time between tasks and trips.
- ★ Make a regular practice of stopping tasks far enough in advance to start preparation for the next task *early*.
- ★ Set all alarms 30 mins earlier than needed so you can leave time for slowing down AND being on time.

October

8

I Speak with CONFIDENCE

We associate speaking with confidence to a person's presentation skills. While confidence is essential when presenting to an audience, let's focus our discussion here on speaking with confidence when having difficult conversations.

Depending on your personality type, confrontation may not be easy. For some, it's easier just to let it go despite how you feel, or even worse, you may never speak to that person again! I had to laugh at myself when writing this because I was once that person!

There are a few things you can do to feel more confident when having a difficult conversation.

★ First, take the emotion out if it. Just focus on the facts.

★ Take some time to reflect and then move to the next step which would be to come up with possible solutions to the conversation.

★ Imagine how you would like the conversation to go with solution-oriented thinking. A win-win scenario would be the best possible outcome. In order for this to happen you have to humble yourself.

★ This means, listen more and talk less. Try to see the where the other person is coming from.

★ The last thing is to know your audience. This may be the most important step.

★ If the person is not ready to have the conversation, give them time.

Hopefully, at the end of your conversation the issue will be resolved, but if it happens that you can't agree, still provide grace and find the beauty in the differences.

— Cortney D. Surrency, AC-CHC

October

I Will Speak Success

"Death and life are in the power of the tongue: and they that love it shall eat the fruit thereof."

Proverbs 18:21 KJV

Words have power. They reveal our thoughts and the matters of the heart, but they also frame our thoughts by creating them, shaping them, and reinforcing them. Words are tools of communication; they are bridges of expression that convey messages. They bring consequences—good or bad.

When you speak, choose well. Choose life. Speak success. Speaking success means having intentionally positive conversations with yourself, about yourself, and the circumstances you will face along the journey. Speaking success means verbalizing the vision board of your future. Speaking success means rehearsing out loud what God says about who you are, what you have, and what you are capable of doing.

Speaking success meanings remembering scriptures like, "You are able because you can do all things through Christ who strengthens you.[7] ALL of your needs are supplied.[8]

---

[7] Philippians 4:13
[8] Philippians 4:19

NOTHING is impossible.[9] God is doing a great work in you, and through you, so you will NOT fail.[10]

Success is yours when you realize that your Creator has deemed you victorious *already*. As they said in ancient biblical terminology, gird up your loins and march on! in today's vernacular: Queen! Square your shoulders! Adjust your crown, and keep moving. Declare victory! Proclaim and expect the great, then walk YE in it!!! ☺

— Dr. Latisha D. Reeves Henry

October

" I Will Uplift. . . without Putting Anyone Down! "

What kind of woman is uplifting while putting others down in the SAME breath?! Why spend time dimming someone else's light so yours shines a bit brighter? Tuh!

When we're focused on OUR core values, we really don't have time to worry our minds about where other people are lacking. Worried about who is not supporting us, what someone is jealous of, or what someone is not doing for us... UGH! Sometimes, we focus on what she's wearing, what event she's not attending, or the "fake" love being shown. Ohhhh YES! We do it—it happens! I hate to admit it. We're human. But when we find ourselves doing this, let's acknowledge it and immediately shift our focus!

Your tribe will come to you by way of your passion when you are being your AUTHENTIC self, so... less depending on what other folks are doing to make YOUR world go around, or you'll be disappointed often!!! Not because people don't care, but

---

[9] Luke 18:27
[10] Philippians 1:6

because people have their own lives, and you never know what folks have occupying THEIR lives, their time, and their mind.

Take care of you and yours, and if you're truly doing this, you will be too preoccupied with UPLIFTING to be putting anyone down!

— Monique Carter

October

I Am Humble

Humility is sign of strength
Humility encourages Love
Humility is graceful
Humility is favored of God
I am Humble and strong
I am gracefully humbled
I'm not passive but passionately humble
I am courageous and humble
I achieve success with humility
My trials have made me humble
I am humble enough to forgive
I am humble and wise
I am humble

God opposes the proud
but gives grace to the Humble

James 4:6

— *Kelly Gardner*

Say Aloud: **I Am Humble!**

October
12

No Need to Compete with Others.
I Am Only Competing with ME!

Passion driven individuals don't have time and energy to waste analyzing their "competitors." Instead, they are using their time and energy pursuing their passion. When you are focused, the only competition you should see is yourself. Focus your energy on bettering your best—not beating "competitors"—and you will probably go much further.

— Erika Harp

October
13

I Will Never Walk A Day in Your Shoes.
I Do My BEST to BOSS in My Own!

My life's experiences have shaped me into the woman I am today, and I am so proud of her. No one truly knows everything about me or what I am truly made of... My life is the most important corporation I will ever run, and I am the BOSS of this corporation—I wouldn't have it any other way!

I've learned to embrace all MY life's ups, downs, twists, and turns. I've learned to seek out the lessons and the blessings. Once I discover my lessons, I place them in my mental book of knowledge and press forward that much stronger and wiser. As a stronger and wiser woman, I'm able to take on life's next "heavy hit." I may stumble, but this time, I won't fall.

I'm super mom to my kids, an awesome wife to my husband, the world's best sister to my brothers, a humble leader among my colleagues, and that friend that ignites those who know me. This is how I BOSS in my shoes, and... No sister! I will never, nor will I ever want to, walk a day in yours.

— Monique Carter

October

" I Will Not Let Outside Opinions Hinder Me "

The opinions of others can hinder you if you let them. Outside opinions can affect the entire essence of who you are to be. the opinions of others can strip you of your joy, sanity, and identity. Opinions can taint your spirit. As a woman, we often focus on our failures and mishaps in life. the unsolicited thoughts of others don't help at all. Together, these things cripple our ability to rejoice in truth.

Take some time to self-reflect and get to know who you are. Understand the essence of who you are. Discover who you were created to be. Be open to evolving, learning new things, and meeting new people. Remember, you are the apple of God's eye! Therefore, God's vision should be front and center in your life—not the opinions of those who don't love you like God does. Allow the voice of God to be a driving force to motivate, cultivate, and accelerate you through life.

AFFIRM:

I Will Not Let Outside Opinion Hinder Me. I will sift through the opinions of others to glean from that which is beneficial and discard those things that are toxic. I will surround myself with conversations that are motivating and uplifting. I will conscientiously protect my space and diligently feed my spirit and mind.

I Will Live in my TRUTH Unapologetically.

I Will Not Let Outsiders Hinder Me!

— Regina N Roberts

October

"I Play the Game with My Own Rules"

I was told that the game has changed
Supposed to spread your legs yet they barely know your name

No commitment at all, but ya'll "keeping it real"
Giving all your gud loving, but he can't pay one bill?

He gives a long list of texts with no conversation
Got a long list of responsibilities with no motivation

You hit him with the question, "What's it gonna be?"
That's when you find out you were just 1 of about 3

this new game is strange; the rules are made up as you go
and even the Queens are being approached like we don't know
(Huh?)

the men want to be pursued because the game pieces are plenty
and not only that, most women do not require any

hard work from these men before they Netflix and chill
a sweet word, some quick texts, then you're 'giving him
something he can feel'

these new Xbox 1 games, I just can't play
I am a vintage Nintendo so our controllers won't connect
anyway

faster is not better, and your update still has glitches
your 3.0 game can't separate the Queens from the witches

so I'll let ya'll make the moves and watch from the side
until I meet the right man whose rules are like mine

— Kwanza Yates

16

Sometimes, Keeping It Real Means Keeping It Real Quiet

If only we would *all* learn this, the world would rotate a lot better. When we gain the understanding that we don't always have to talk or respond to things, we would get more done and have more peace.

Learn to observe and be quiet. Resist the urge to react to everything. Discern when to speak, and when not to and your stress will be minimized, irritation lowered, frustration eliminated, and aggravation would be limited. Telling it like it is doesn't make you real. Wisdom does. It is okay *not* to speak about everything. It is okay *not* to have an opinion about all things. It is alright to keep things to *yourself*.

Speaking too much can kill your witness. It can cause people to veer away from wanting your input.

Kill your ego. You don't have to have a response to everything.

— Coach Latoya Kight

October

17

I Will Come Out of My Shell. . .

I will come out of my shell. I will continue to increase my confidence and self-esteem. I will no longer allow my past experiences to keep me bound, trapped, and fearful. I will step outside of my comfort zone. I will not settle in complacency nor settle for mediocrity—in myself or in others. I will speak up more, say what is on my mind, and share my thoughts. I will lift my head up high and speak with assurance and clarity. I will take on new experiences, visit new places, meet new people, and take on new projects even when I am afraid. I will stop dimming my light in fear of making others uncomfortable.

This is ofttimes our own delusion, and if in fact, someone is uncomfortable, this has more to do with how they feel about themselves than with how they feel about us. This is when we stop worrying about what people think of us. *(Believe it or not, people are not as interested in us as we think they are.)*

So...

...move...

...move with grace.

Move with humility. Keep God first and watch Him work in your life.

— Monique Carter

October

" Trying to Fit in Ensures I Never Stand Out "

I had a conversation with someone once. They stated how they realized that most of the younger generation—*including me*—was trying so hard to be original, but everyone was doing the same exact things. Now... you ladies know, for young people, everything is about what's trending. Being a popular topic seems to be the only way to be accepted by peers, but that's only if you are doing something that's trending.

Here, I'll propose something different: Why be afraid to go against the grain? It is not my desire to fit in because if I am fitting in with the things that others are doing, I am most likely operating outside the realm of my purpose. Christ calls us to be set apart—to be different. People may not understand why you decided to wait for marriage to have sex or why you can't go to the parties anymore. They may not understand why you changed the way you dress or why you changed your circle of friends or your choice of music. Christ calls us to be set apart, so if you are aiming to fit in as a Christian woman, you are off the mark. Besides, trying to fit in ensures you never stand out.

— Kenajawa LaShawn

October

"I FIT: I Am the Perfect Fit"

We, as women, wear so many hats. We are mothers, daughters, sisters, friends, lovers, caregivers, educators, nurturers, and so much more. I fit into all of these roles effortlessly. Now my jeans??? Different story! It amazes me how fluid we are as women, juggling all of these different responsibilities, transitioning from one to another without effort.

Women... you are so beautiful to watch, comforting the baby after he falls down and scrapes his knee, swooping in to the rescue to make him feel safe. Care is so second nature to you that I don't believe that it even requires thought. You quickly glide into action, and faith in humanity is once again restored.

You and I are the perfect fit and are still so unique in our own rights. That is what is so beautiful about us... no two of us are the same... no two talents exact. Spiritual gifts that were hand selected for each of us... no two carried out in a carbon copy way because we are the same, yet we are individual and so unique... That makes us the perfect fit!

— Stephanie Hamilton Muwunganirwa

October

"

I AM the Exception

John Maxwell discusses a law of difference which states that "the more different you are, the more difference you make." the first time I heard this, it made my whole LIFE make sense! I was *always* different, and it never made sense to me why I couldn't just be like everyone else.

Oftentimes, in a world where everyone is trying to blend in, it is difficult to embrace the fact that you are different. You are uniquely made, and you *should* stand out from the crowd. It's okay to be who you are; it's okay to look how you look; it's okay to embrace the fact that you are different. You are the answer to a problem in this world, and THAT makes you different. You are a "difference-maker!"

Many great inventions have been created because someone saw things differently. If you attempt to be like everyone else, the world will never get to experience what *you* have that only *you* can give. You ARE the exception!!! You have the ability to break the rules and become EXACTLY what they said you couldn't be! You can do what they said you couldn't do, and complete what they said you can't complete, all because you ARE the exception! You can do what they said was impossible... YOU... are the exception—the exception to your situation and the exception to your circumstances. Don't be afraid to be the difference. Don't be afraid to break the rules! You can do what has never been done. No one is like you! Don't be afraid to be the exception.

— Coach Mechelle Canady

Say Aloud: **I AM the Exception.**

October

"

Sticks and Stones
May Break My Bones, But....
Words Hurt Too!

"

Growing up, the elder folks would say, "Words will never hurt you," or, "It's not what they call you, it's what you answer to." Let's not forget old faithful, "Who cares what people think?" After a while, I found out, we do care! Rightfully so! We're human, and words do hurt.

Let us be mindful of how impactful our words can be. Words have the power to make a sunny day cloudy or to turn a rainy day into sunshine. Once we release words, we can never take them back. We must speak carefully and be intentional with our conversations, all while being honest and unafraid to have difficult discussions. Consider this with all your relationships and encounters: ask yourself, "Is what I'm about to say going to discourage or encourage? Will my words make a positive difference in this situation? Who will be impacted by these words, and how? Will the people in my presence be better or worse after the conversations we've held?"

Speak words of kindness no matter the situation and watch your words build bridges that you never thought to be possible.

— Monique Carter

Say Aloud: **I Will Speak Words of Kindness.**

There is POWER in My Words!

There is power in your words. Proverbs 18:21 says, "Death and life are in the power of the tongue and they that love it shall eat the fruit." the scripture is saying that you eat the fruit of what your tongue speaks. If your tongue speaks positive, your fruit will be positive. If your tongue speaks negative, your fruit will be negative. the power of this affirmation is in the knowledge that you can speak good things into existence, and you can speak life into a dead situation.

In the Bible, God told Isaiah to speak to the dry bones; he spoke to the bones, and they came back together and lived. *What situation in your life do you need to speak to?* Speaking life will change how your situation looks and determine how it ends.

Mothers, we need to speak positively into the lives of our children. We should speak things to them regarding how great they are until they are **convinced** of it! Speak positivity over their lives until they believe who they are, and then... speak it even more! Even for yourself, if there's something you're not believing in, start to speak positively and watch these seeds begin to grow.

Our words have life! Our words have power! Today, start speaking positively! Speak LIFE because there is power in your tongue.

— Coach Mechelle Canady

I Will Say No Firmly

For some, saying "No" is a challenging task. Saying no can lead to anger, disappointment, or frustration in others. However, saying no can also lead to understanding or compassion.

Our lives are eventful, and we have a lot of responsibilities on our plates. As much as we may desire to add another task to our workload, additional items can be overwhelming. It is important to say "No," and to say it firmly. Saying no with confidence will help the other person to take you more seriously. If you are coy about saying no, this may provoke others to continue to ask you for assistance or may provoke others to take advantage of you. If there is someone who knows you always say yes, they are going to continue to ask you for favors. Why wouldn't they?

Learn to say no with assurance. You don't want to overwhelm yourself while trying to influence the happiness of others. When saying no, be confident in your decision. This is all easier said than done, but over time, saying no will begin to grow easier.

—— Arielle Griffin

Say Aloud: **I Will Say No Firmly!**

October

" I Set Healthy Boundaries with Myself and Others "

It can be tough setting healthy boundaries with others, and it can be even harder setting boundaries with yourself! We find ourselves very busy being problem solvers for others, and at the end of the day, you have nothing left to give to yourself.

Think of your time, tears, thoughts, money, and love as a rope. Every time someone asks of you, they pull away at your rope. If your rope is not protected, it could eventually be left with a single thread. You have an obligation to yourself to protect your rope even if the abuser is a loved one. Stop thinking that you're selfish and start acting selfless! Start doing things that will add to your rope like going to the beach or a getting mani-pedi. I would encourage you to start hanging out with people that only want your company and need nothing in return from you.

Write down five things (or people) that pull away from your rope and start practicing how to lovingly say, "No," or "Let me think about it." Replace those five things with five things (or people) that will add to your rope and start saying, "Yes!"

— Cortney D. Surrency, AC-CHC

October

" I Am A True Friend "

True friends are hard to come by. Being a true friend means that you're genuine in all aspects of life. There should not be any question of your loyalty when you are a true friend.

While being a true friend, you must always consider how your friends will feel in situations. You must always consider if your actions are negatively affecting your friend. If you can't be honest or you can't be positive with your comrade, you are not a true friend. If your comrade has to question your loyalty, you are not a true friend. If your comrade has to question whether you're trustworthy, you're not a true friend.

It takes a lot to be a true friend. You have to be unselfish. You have to have empathy and sympathize with your friends. A true friend is an ear and a confidante, so a true friend keeps their mouth closed. A true friend is a vault that will never open.

Stay true even in disagreement.

Your word is your bond, so stay consistent.

— Coach Latoya Kight

October

" I Won't Be the Root of Gossip "

Often, we take pride in knowing something about one woman that others may not know. We enjoy being the first person another woman runs to when a situation hits the fan. We sit on the phone and talk about the latest TEA—the latest, "Girl! Have you heard about sister so and so?" OR "If I was her, I wouldn't..." OR, my favorite, "If it was me, I would." Well, guess what? It's not you! *(At least this time it isn't.)*

Please believe, if you participate in gossip, when it's your turn to be the subject of the day, these same people will show you just as much mercy as you showed towards your sisters.

We have all heard that "when someone brings you a bone, they have their spit on it too." This means that when you get the latest juicy tale, something has already been added, taken out, and exaggerated, but... we still listen. Today, choose not to be a trash can—don't allow people to bring you garbage. If you overhear some gossipy nonsense about another woman, keep quiet! Ask yourself, "Am I my sister's keeper?" That's the question of the day, and yes, my dear...

...you are!

— Chantell Williams

October

"

I Will Lead

"

I will lead others by modeling my belief in leadership.
I will lead others in ways that will stretch them to be better versions of themselves.
I will lead by grace.
I will lead in love.
I will lead through the exposure of my own walk of faith, love, prayer, and community.
I will lead in truth.
I will lead by sharing the spotlight and creating a safe place for others.
I will lead through the struggle.
I will lead in peace, discipline, respect, and through modeling that which is noble.

— Regina N Roberts

I Will Be A Better Mother

Minutes quickly turn to hours that flow into days and weeks are a blur as the months pass. Before I know it, all the times I've taken for granted have now come and gone, so I try to live more in the moment and find joy in life's minor inconveniences.

It's easy to let those precious moments slip by in our busy lives with so many things on our plate. It's easy to brush by those little things that matter so much to my child. She looks up to me and always wants to do what mommy does, so I try to be better in all ways—just for her. I try to be more patient and let her help me cook. I am slow to get angry over minor mishaps, remembering, "She is human, and she will make mistakes."

I am kind to others, and I can see the impact this has had on her. She is learning to become a woman from me, so my job is to be the best woman I can be because, at the end of the day, my child is who I do it all for.

— Brittany Whigham

Say Aloud: **I Will Be A Better Mother!**

October
29

“

I Do More, And I Am More

”

Do wonderful things that make you feel good about yourself! Do them, so you feel accomplished! Enjoy your surroundings and travel the world. Do more than shop... explore! Shopping is a temporary gratification. It creates an addictive high. We must be about more than shoes and purses. Don't get me wrong: I love purses, shoes, make-up, and clothes. They help contribute to my beauty, but when we make our looks create the foundation of who we are, then we are selling ourselves so very short.

Big butt and large breasts... if all you bring to the table are looks, what substance does that provide? You must also have wisdom and intelligence, which means you need to be well-read, knowledgeable, and experienced. You must be intuitive, which means you are in tune with who you are and all the wonderful and unique things that make you who you are. You must try your very best to do better in every way, and when you start doing more, you will find yourself being more.

— Kwanza Yates

October
30

“

I Will Break the Cycles...

”

I will break the cycles for my daughters to know what they are getting into. I will break the cycles of silence that we as women have lived through. I will share my stories with my daughters so they can share their stories with their daughters someday. My daughters aren't biologically mine, but it's necessary for me to talk to them about everything that wasn't told to me that I had to figure out on my own. My mother is a beautiful woman who I aspire to be like. However, she left a lot to chance after I started my period. I wouldn't say she checked out, but my sex talk was literally, "It's just something going in and out." *If it didn't happen that way, at least that's how I remember it.*

When their periods started, my daughters came to me in the most humbling way. My middle daughter started at ten. Her older sister started at age eleven, and when Francisca—my youngest daughter—started, I came home from work one day, and she said, "Mommy, something bad happened today." Being concerned, I asked, "What happened?" She said, "I have blood coming out my lady parts." Needless to say, my daughters and will talk through whatever.

The first time my Mom had cancer, I learned when she was preaching to the congregation. I was in that congregation. It hurt that I didn't know prior. *She'll swear I didn't listen. However, that's not the case.* My girls took care of her, and of course, we talked through it all. Together, we will continue to have these uncomfortable conversations and others. Together, we will work to break the cycles of silence in our family. I hope you can do the same with yours.

— Stephanie Hamilton Muwunganirwa

Say Aloud: **I Will Break the Cycles...**

October

I Will Share My Story

I will share my story.

I will share how he took advantage of me when I was younger and thought that forcing a few dollars in my hand made it better. I will share how my mother loved her drugs more than she loved me, so growing up, I never knew what her face looked like. I will share how my father spelled his love across my body with bruises. I will share how I made it to college with a full-ride scholarship but failed my first year. I will share how I had a stillborn child at age 20. I will share how I allowed three different men to take advantage of me without standing up for myself. I will also share how I tried to end my life five times because I didn't feel that I was worth living.

Why will I share my story?

Because someone like you may need to hear it...

You may need to hear that I made it through. You made need to know that I am still surviving. You made need to know that by forgiving all the people that have hurt me in the past, I have found freedom in the present. You may need to hear how, by finding my relationship with God, I was able to find love, peace, value, and identity. I will continue to share my story because I know that by hearing the stories of others, I was able to find hope. If my story has the chance of helping at least one person, I will continue to share my story.

— Kenajawa LaShawn

Partnership & Sisterhood

November 1

"I Love My Sisters"

Yeeeeeeees, I absolutely love y'all!!

From the sister stranger that blesses me with her words of encouragement to the sister that swears and rolls her eyes at me for reasons unknown to me, I LOVE YOU!! From the sister stranger with the "Yeeeeees, hair!!!" compliment to the childhood friend that knows my deepest secrets, I LOVE YOU!!

— Erika Harp

November 2

"I Will Listen to the Secrets of My Sisters"

I will listen to the secrets of my sisters and create a space that welcomes and soothes their vulnerabilities.

I will listen to my sister in a space and time that shares feedback and propels her to move forward in faith and assurance. I will listen to my sisters without judgment and abandonment.

I will listen to my sister in the spirit of grace.

I will listen to my sisters in times of disagreement and offer forgiveness and reconciliation.

I will listen to the secrets of my sisters that houses their most vulnerable hearts of the matter and rightly seek justice on their behalf.

A faithful friend is a sturdy shelter
He that has found me Has found a treasure
Ecclesiasticus 6:14

— Regina N Roberts

November 3

" I Will Not Keep All of My Secrets to Myself "

Have you ever wondered why secrets exist?

Think about all the things that should have been spoken of and shared to help free you and others.

As a child, I was highly encouraged to believe that not talking was always the best course of action. in my silence, I was only able to observe things that were happening to me and around me. As an adult, I've often struggled with knowing the right time to share, if I should share, and who to share with. This became extremely exhausting and heavy.

In my twenties, I was introduced to the blessing of sharing. Although I was fearful of what would happen when I shared my secrets, sharing created relief that warmed my heart and soul. As I experienced life, sharing my own secrets became freeing. This freedom allowed me to be cared for by others. This freedom brought relief in my mind, body, and spirit.

Having and keeping secrets holds you captive and keeps you from living a life that is fulfilled and joyous. Free yourself and no longer be bound by your silence. There is someone in this world who is worth sharing your secrets with. If you haven't found that person yet, it's probably because you haven't shared enough of yourself with the world.

— Regina N Roberts

Say Aloud: **I Will Not Keep My Secrets to Myself!**

" I Will Uplift Her and Clap When She Wins. We Are STRONGER Together! "

Women uplifting and supporting other women is becoming more and more of a reality every day. We are beginning to realize we ARE stronger together—that a simple "Girl, you got this!" can go a long way! She is *not* your competition. She is your sister! She is who you are speaking to in all your inspirational quotes, videos, and posts, right?! So, when she begins to win, shine, and rise... let's keep that same energy of support! Continue to be that push and anchor she needed; she may need it even more so now that she's really shining in her greatness!

Send encouragement to your sister when she wins! Everyone, including you, will have their time to shine. You have no idea what defines success for her, the work she puts in behind the scenes or the sacrifices she makes daily. Clap when you see another woman win! She may or may not have the same obstacles or came from a similar upbringing. She could have thrown in the towel because life has given her so many reasons to do so yet... she still makes it through! You're both winners, yet you're running very different races. Celebrate with your sister, show her love, congratulate her, and collaborate on ways you can BOTH keep getting better. We're all unique in our gifts, talents, strengths, and challenges, and this is a GOOD thing because we can do better together! We are stronger together!

— Monique Carter

Say Aloud: I Uplift Her and Clap When She Wins!

November 5

" I Champion the Wins of My Sisters "

In life, sometimes others will win in an area before you do. Don't be upset or down about it. Celebrate them! Be SO amped that you're able to celebrate with them as if it is your win. Genuinely cheer for your sister. Be excited! Be happy! Don't hold back the joy you feel. Let your sister know how thrilled you are for her. That way, you will be next.

God will bless you tremendously because of your pure heart for another's elevation. Help the people around you rise, and you will follow. Shout it out to others! Brag about it! It is always okay to marvel at what others have obtained or accomplished.

It takes too much work to be mad, jealous, or hurt about someone else winning. Be the host of their party. Don't be the party pooper.

— Coach Latoya Kight

November 6

" I Will Be A Better Friend "

As we each grow and mature, changes occur, and our lives are suddenly so busy and full. I remember anxiously anticipating weekends that my friends and I could hang out. We did everything—*and nothing*—

together, but with all that life throws at you, sometimes we forget about those friends, those bonds, and how special both truly are.

As time passes, our new lives and responsibilities strain those relationships that were once so close. We tend to walk away from those bonds because things have changed, but as life moves and evolves, we must adapt. Although we may not be able to hang out all the time, a simple call or text—to let that friend know they've crossed our mind—can mean a lot.

Be sure to reach out and support the efforts of those old friends in any way possible. Whether the connection is professional, personal, or spiritual, your friends would love hearing from you. Love is an action, so choose to show more love to those who have chosen to love you.

— Brittany Whigham

November 7

I Will Pay It Forward

We stand on the shoulders of our mothers, our grandmothers, and great grandmothers. We walk through doors they dreamed about even though they may never get the opportunity to see the fruits of their labor. We live where we want. We work where we want. We drive what we want, and even marry who we want. We have options because these women sacrificed for us. These women thought it not robbery to step out of what is considered "the normal" and created a whole new world of opportunity.

Will the next woman be you? Will you think the unthinkable? Will you do the unexplainable? Will you go above and beyond so some woman can stand on your shoulders?

See, we always think paying it forward is buying food for the lady in line behind us. That is one way to see it, but I challenge you to think higher!

I'll see you on the other side Queen.

— Chantell Williams

November 8

" I Will Not Rain on the Parade of Other Women!!! "

I will not rain on the parade of other women. Instead, I will join in on their parade. I will join another woman's unification of what she possesses. I will join a woman sharing ideas, creating life, and birthing purpose. I will join a woman providing newness and free life by creating plausible solutions. This woman is identifying her own strengths, her weaknesses and sharing special moments in life with others. I join the parade because when I win another woman wins. When I win, women are happy. When women win, we all win.

If women understood and exercised their power, they could remake the world.

Emily Taft Douglas

— LeLeatha Mitchell

November

I Support Other Women

Supporting other women comes so natural to me. We are all so unique in our gifts—it's like our own superpower! We tend to forget that no two people are 100% alike, and we can all teach and learn from one another. There is enough in this world for all of us to win at *something*.

It is essential to my growth and genuine curiosity that I surround myself with women who openly "appreciate" other women.

You ever hear another woman say, "I just don't do women?" It's so interesting to hear this come from ...a woman! It's interesting—to say the least—and though you may be the one to change minds, it may not be in your best interest to invest too much time in women who simply don't "do" you. *(It can be draining and downright confusing.)*

Instead of spending all your good energies in negative places, show love and uplift the women in your life who will appreciate and grow from it—like the flowers we are! Show love by exchanging knowledge and ideas, by collaborating, and by investing in one another's projects or businesses. Support other women by being a mentor or a safe place for your fellow sisters.

Use your voice to speak good and hold those courageous conversations with and for others. Do this wholeheartedly, and it will come back to you tenfold.

— Monique Carter

Say Aloud: **I Support Other Women!**

November 10

Don't Let Comparison Stop Your Creativity!

Creatives...

You owe it to yourself to live free from the box that is placed around your gift. Some people eat, drink, and live in the boxes they've been placed in every day while others do not. Do you really believe that your sister is better because she has a different gift than you? Do you believe she is better because she has a better gift than the one you desire? She is not better than you! Maybe she simply works at her craft more, or perhaps it's just her time to shine.

We have to be honest about our comparisons because, many times, they block us from being more, and truly, they block us from being honest. Did you put in the hours you needed? Did you study as you should have? Did you take your goal seriously enough to invest in it like you've seen some others do? Think about it. How can a painter call herself an artist if she never bought a brush???

You can be anything you want to be, but you have to want it bad enough and do the work. Your display of creativity in your area of expertise could be the next big thing, so let's get to work Queen! Don't let comparison stop your creativity!

— Chantell Williams

Say Aloud: Comparison Won't Stop My Creativity!

I Have Learned That to Truly Be Blessed I Must First Be A Blessing

Blessing others boils down to humility, and having humility is about having an 'it's not about me' attitude. Blessing others is not about the blessing that is received at all; it's about having the heart to serve others because of the sacrifice that has been made for us. Even if the blessing I feel is not tangible, there is a feeling that's left in my spirit when I know I have done something to bless another. This happens when I share a smile or a kind word. It happens when I pay it forward by buying someone's lunch.

There are always needs that must be met around us. I believe that just by being more outwardly focused, we can be a blessing much more often than we think. Being a true blessing is not about receiving something in return, but rather, it's about what can be done to go the extra mile for those around you.

How can you do something different today to be a blessing to someone?

— Kenajawa LaShawn

Say Aloud: to **Be Blessed, I Must Be A Blessing**

November 12

I Will Perform Acts of Service

Performing acts of service can prove to be very fulfilling. Being there for others, and helping when needed, provides blessings to all involved. An act of service can be traveling to a foreign country to complete a mission trip. It can also be providing those who are experiencing homelessness with a warm meal. Spending a Saturday volunteering for a cause near to your heart can be so eye-opening. This level of selflessness can impact your life in a positive way.

I believe that when you send positive energy into the world, you receive it back, so volunteer your time and bring friends along. Time is valuable, but it is well spent when you are using it to help others.

Make a goal to perform at least two acts of service a month. Pass these traits to your children and allow them to see you leaving a positive footprint on the world. Through your continued acts of service, you have the power to influence many.

— Arielle Griffin

Say Aloud: **I Will Perform Acts of Service**

" I Will Walk with Women Who EMBRACE Me! "

We give other people too much power over our minds when we get tripped up on what they say is normal or not normal.! How can you show your individuality if you're constantly trying to be someone or something else? Who told you that individuality was wrong? Who told you it's not time? Who told you that you aren't good enough? Who told you it couldn't be done? Who told you it's not big enough? Who told you no? Hmmm?? Who told you???

Well, *they* don't have any power over you and your outcomes unless you give it to them! Step over all the people who can't see and support your vision. Instead, show it to the women who knew you could get it done all along. Put more positive women in your corner. Use them as a sounding board to work out your plans. There's no need to walk in a circle of women who can't see what you *can* do because they're busy looking for all that you can't do. If you embrace women who believe in you, they will embrace you in return, and once you've got them in your corner, you will soon begin to embrace and realize your dreams!

— Chantell Williams

Affirmation Journal
* ★ How supportive am I of others?
* ★ How supportive am I of myself?
* ★ In what ways will I embrace others in the future?

Say Aloud: **I Will Walk with Women Who EMBRACE Me!**

I Will Show Love to Other Women!!!

I will show love to other women in the way I build relationships with other women. I will share in the joys, tears, and laughter of other women. I will show love to other women when in the FIGHT of my life and theirs. I will show love to other women in my desire to be a sister and friend, a companion, and a partner. I will show love to other women with a simple hug, a shoulder to support them, words of kindness, and grace to build them up. I will show love to other women with honesty and loyalty. I will show love to other women by modeling excellence, vulnerability, and love!

I challenge you to connect with other women. Seek out a strong woman for mentorship. Offer companionship to one another and connect with others through prayer and praise. Help other women find their place of peace.

— Regina N Roberts

I Will Share Love with Other Women

I recall one day leaving work after having a terrible day. the worries of life were piling up, and I couldn't take it anymore. I knew that when I went home, I was going to end my life. I laid in my bed and cried, thinking about how I would end it.

My phone rang...

...it was my mentor.

I debated answering the call, but somehow, I ended up answering it. I silenced my tears and cleared my voice to mask my current emotions. She called for something unrelated but ended up asking me how I was doing. I couldn't hold it in any longer—everything came pouring out.

That day, she called for nothing in particular, just to see how I was doing.

That moment of love saved my life!

> *Love is patient, love is kind.*
> *It does not envy, it does not boast,*
> *it is not proud.*
> *It is not rude, it is not self-seeking,*
> *it is not easily angered,*
> *it keeps no record of wrongs.*
> *Love does not delight in evil*
> *but rejoices with the truth.*
> *It always protects, always trusts,*
> *always hopes, always perseveres.*
> *Love never fails.*
>
> *1 Corinthians 13:4*

After understanding what love really is by experiencing the ultimate love of God, I was able to understand how I should love others—ESPECIALLY MY SISTERS! for all women I encounter, I vow to be the image of God's love. While the world is aiming to tear us down, we must be willing to build each other up! So, go out of your way to show someone a little extra love each day. Smile at the next woman you pass. Buy a co-worker lunch. Text that person that's been on your heart—let them know you are thinking of them.

A little love can go a long way.

— Kenajawa LaShawn

November 16

" I Will Show Myself to Be A Friend "

Luke 6:31 says, "Do to others as you would have them do to you."

Be the friend you desire to have. If you want to be friends with others, you must first show yourself to be the kind of friend that you want. You can't possibly want to have positive relationships when you are not displaying (or welcoming) the traits of the friend that you would like. Change your negative demeanor into a positive one. Change your aura into a good one. If it's negative, change your outlook into a positive one so you can receive friends.

Don't lose the opportunity to be a friend by being stuck in your habits and stuck in the way that you want to be. Compromise. Change the way you see things and change the way you operate when it comes to friendships, so you can have the fulfilling and amazing relationships that you desire.

You are what you attract, so be mindful of the fact that you are attracting things that represent you in some way. If you want to attract goodness, be good. If you want to attract love, be loving. Always be willing to change some things about yourself to fit the mold of what you want to be around. This takes sacrifice, so start changing some dynamics about your life and show yourself to be a friend.

— Coach Latoya Kight

Affirmation Journal

★ When was the last time I showed myself to be a friend?

★ How often do I show my friendship to others?

★ Who, in my life, needs to know that I care about them?

November

I Will Find A Squad

Having someone or a few people that are on your spiritual wavelength is so important throughout this thing we call life. You need a system of people who won't judge your past or where you are right now in your life—people who will encourage you even when you feel like giving up. When you have a real squad, you can confidently trust the advice they give you and can use them as a sounding board to receive confirmation on a situation or a gut feeling.

So, how do you know if your squad is legit?

The first thing to assess is their connection with God. If their vertical connection (to God) is strong, then their horizontal connection with you will be stronger. They will give you advice not of their own, but they will share what the Holy Spirit shares through them to you.

The second sign is knowing and appreciating each other's spiritual gifts. That is so crucial to the friendship. I find that you benefit from each other's spiritual gifts during a time of need and confirmation. Spiritual gifts between friends can also be highly compatible!

Lastly, if you find that you can tell them anything— I mean anything—where you can't help it and you *know with all your heart that they will protect the information, then you have found your squad.*

— Cortney D. Surrency, AC-CHC

November 18

I Will Ask for Help

Throughout life, asking for help has been very difficult to do for me. I wish I had made this declaration years ago. Life would have been easier. However, I finally got to a point where I learned to change my perspective on how I interpreted the need to ask for help. As my perspective has changed, I've been able to go through life with more ease than anxiety. I remember a time in my life when asking for help would stir up anxiety, tears, and frustration. It doesn't have to be that way for you like it was for me.

Asking for help allows people, purpose, and passion into your life. the combination of all of these things brings forth abundant living! Allowing others to provide help ignites a sense of community that shares the gift of giving. Asking for help lightens a heavy load, reduces stress, or anxiety, and it removes the perspective that you are in this world alone.

In my walk with Christ, as I've become more open and willing to ask *Him* for all the things He's promised, I am also now able to ask those around me for the provisions I often prayed for.

Reflect on your own manner of asking. Learn to ask for the things you need and then the things you desire. Understanding your father will provide, learn to view the need to "ask" as a means of resource sharing.

— Regina N Roberts

Say Aloud: **I Will Ask for Help!**

November

I Lead When I Need To.
I Follow When Life Calls for It.

I am a leader.

I am created to be the head and not the tail, so I will always be a leader. I will always go forth with what God has called me to do. I will always lead and not fall into what someone says I should do. I will always lead and not be held back from what I am supposed to do.

I will follow whenever I need to.

I am humble enough to know that I can be a follower and a leader all at the same time. I'm humble enough to know that I don't always have to lead. I don't always have to be in charge. I know that I am a servant at heart so that I can be as well. I don't have to succumb to either one posture or the other—I can balance them both out.

I know that I was called to be a leader, but I also am called to be a servant. I can follow someone else's lead because I don't know the answers to everything. I don't know how to do everything, and I don't know where to go all the time. Sometimes, I have to humble myself and be okay with following someone else. That does not negate who I am as a leader. It doesn't make me less than anyone else. It doesn't change who I am. It doesn't make me small. It makes me wise.

I will always be wise and follow when I need to follow and lead when life calls for it.

— Coach Latoya Kight

I Will Learn from Other Women
While Leading My Own Path to Success

It is important to be your own person throughout life. Don't depend on others for your happiness because only *you* can maintain your happiness. in life, work to create your own path and be confident in the path you create. Following others may take you down the wrong path.

Some women even lead others in the wrong direction intentionally because of jealousy or bad intentions. Be careful of the women you choose to follow, and if you are following another lady... make sure it is for the right reasons. It is okay sometimes to follow a woman because she is a positive influence or role model in your life. *Learning from other women is major!* Yes, sometimes you may follow a woman to learn what has—and has not—worked for her, but make sure you document all that you learn and use it to create your own path.

We don't know everything there is to know, and we can all benefit from life lessons and advice from the women around us. However, in the end, make your own path because leading is instrumental to your success.

— Arielle Griffin

Say Aloud: **I Will Learn from Other Women!**

November 21

I Am BLESSED by My Friends

We are blessed by association!

If you accept this concept, then you would agree that the company you keep could either get you closer to a blessing or further from it! Having friends that are plugged in to God's will can have a profound effect on your life. When you have praying friends, who are full of faith, they believe that nothing happens by chance! They understand that the perfect will of God for their life and the environment that they surround themselves with can spill over in your life.

When your friends are blessed, you are blessed. When God blesses them, you can benefit and vice versa. For Christian women, we have a responsibility to our friends, and even to strangers, to live a righteous life because their own life's blessings could depend on our lifestyle. A project at work can go better than expected because your coworker's obedience and faithfulness could help you look impressive to the boss as well. So, remember that the company you keep is more important than you think!

— Cortney D. Surrency, AC-CHC

Say Aloud: I Am BLESSED by My Friends

" All Women Are Important "

From the stay at home mom to the corporate executive... all women are valuable and have an impact on the world.

Think of all the women who've crossed your path and their direct and indirect impact on your life. Think about your mother and her unconditional love for you, including everything attached to you, such as your children. Think about your grandmother and all her infinite wisdom, tough love, and hilarious honesty. Think about the close friend who became a sister and someone with whom you can share your secrets, your greatest joys, and your fears. What about the aunt who will always have your back or the homemaker who takes pride in maintaining her home through organization, cleanliness, raising children, and supporting her mate? Think about the working moms who share the same internal guilt as you because of her heart to be at home with her children and her desire to be a successful career woman. *What an unending tug-o-war THAT is! SHEESH!* Think about the childless woman who has no desire to bear children. Despite what society tries to push on her, she has chosen to show support and spread her love in other ways. She is the light in the life of her loved ones, and she has the ability and freedom to flow.

Think of ALL of us! We are all teachers—all leaders! We are ALL important! Together, we can learn, and we can grow! We can become the best version of WOMAN that each of us was meant to be.

— Monique Carter

Say Aloud: All Women Are Important!

The Struggle is Real, but so is the Sisterhood.

For the ladies who have real friends… real women who you can pour into and drink from… real females you can discuss with and disagree with… those you can laugh and cry with, scream and support—and if necessary—get a little revenge with *(younger days)*…

Don't you feel blessed to have that in your life?

I feel sorry for men that they don't talk and fellowship as we do. I feel sorry for women who don't know how to be a real friend—those who instead choose to behave as an enemy to women. to any woman who says, "I don't do female friends," I say, "WOW!" Sounds like it's time for some self-evaluation, sister!

For those of you who have found the luck to have even just one sister you can call a friend, share your secrets, tell your heartache, laugh at your foolishness, sit on the phone with for hours, pray with, travel with, have lunch with, share ideas with......Lady, you are abundantly blessed.

I know we all want a man *(for my single ladies)*, but until one shows up, HONOR and CELEBRATE your girlfriends. They are present for a reason. Their honesty can actually help you reveal and heal the very things you try to hide.

— Kwanza Yates

This Woman's Work (Today)

- ☆ List 3 women in your life who have shown you the importance of sisterhood.
- ☆ Take time to write them a nice note.
- ☆ Mail it. Email it. Text it OR Call her! ☺

ALL Women Are BEAUTIFUL!

All women are beautiful in the way they walk.
All women are beautiful in the way they talk.
All women are beautiful in accomplishing the
challenge of motherhood.
All women are beautiful in their perseverance.
All women are beautiful, being able to birth
nations.
All women are beautiful, being able to take an
idea and manifest empires.
All women are
adorning natural beauty,
angelic and soft,
sassy and soulful,
fierce and brave,
charismatic and intelligent.

*Beauty is truth's smile when she beholds
her own face in a perfect mirror.*
Rabindranath Tagore

— Regina N Roberts

Say Aloud: **ALL Women Are BEAUTIFUL!!**

I Cherish My Grandma's Song.
My Female Elders Make Me Strong.

I heard her voice. From the time I was born,
A melody so sweet it filled my heart with calm.
I would hear her footsteps walking near
And eagerly listen for her songs of cheer.
She sang to me when life went wrong.
She sang her songs to make me strong.
When she saw tears in my eyes,
She would sing a song of lullaby.
Grandma's song has a special beat
That makes angels dance on their feet.
In her heart, the rhythm of love echoes.
The words of her song our family knows.
God gave her songs to guide us every day,
They are words of love, peace, and forgiveness
when we pray.

—Minister Gail Engram

Say Aloud: **My Female Elders Make Me Strong!**

I LOVE Other Ladies!

To love other ladies is to embrace other ladies.
To love other ladies is to share in the lives of other ladies.
To love other ladies is to take a woman under your wing and invest.
Invest in other ladies through word, thought, and deed.
To love other ladies is to protect and cover them.
Love other ladies because their esteem depends on it.
Love other ladies because, in every lady, there is a small reflection of you.
Loving on other ladies gives the opportunity to share in her victories and failures.
Love on other ladies even when they fall, disappoint, and reject you.
Through love, learn to pray, praise, and make peace with other ladies.

Let us always meet each other with smile,
for the smile is the beginning of love.

Mother Teresa

— Regina N Roberts

Affirmation Journal

★ Why do women *need* my love?
★ How do I express my love for other ladies?
★ How does my love of women help women?
★ How does my love of women help me?
★ How can I express even more love for women?

November 27

Stand TALL as a WOMAN!

Stand tall in your skin next to the women with the dark hair
whose lips are full and whose hips are round.
She is love in every capacity you can imagine—even in the
parts of your mind that cannot imagine her love.

Stand tall in your skin next to the woman
who put her dreams on hold to raise her children
for she is the sacrifice of a woman.

Stand tall in your skin next to the woman who works in
corporate America,
for she a symbol of hope that we can do anything.

Stand tall in the grace of a woman and how she moves
throughout the day,
for she is a staple,
and you can't get around her.
She is forgiveness wrapped in strength,
and even if you scratch her,
she will find a way to heal.

She is victorious, and everything she touches turns to gold.

Stand tall in your skin no matter what color it may be
because we are all *beautiful* in our own way.

— Chantell Williams

November 28

" Tall Girls Do Not Be Afraid to Wear Heels "

With every stride you take, make sure you take a few steps in a pair of heels. in accentuating your look, remember that heels are just as important as your handbags *(and if you are a woman like me, you have almost 100 pair)*. From kitten heels to six inches or better, girl… you better walk! If you don't know how to strut your stuff in your heels, get together with a girlfriend who does and ask her for help.

Whether you actually wear heels or not, the goal here is to make sure you always look your best from head to *shoe*. Your heels can make or break an outfit altogether, so why not slay with your best pair? If you are 5'8" or taller, this is especially true for you! Don't cut down your heels or avoid them! Girl! Walk TALL like an Amazon woman! the earth is yours, so with every step you take, make sure you take it in your *best* pair of heels!

You know, they say dogs are a man's best friend. Well, shoes are a woman's best friend! You better walk! *Don't be afraid!*

— Chantell Williams

This Woman's Work (This Week)

* Consider a young lady in your network who could use a bit of mentorship and guidance from you.
* Reach out to her and ask if she'd be interested in working more closely with you.
* Schedule time for your first formal connection.
* Before the week is out, plan the next 6 connections that you all will make.
* Help this woman stand TALL in her heels in LIFE! ☺

I Will BOLDLY Let My Light Shine.
I Will Live OUT LOUD!

Don't let anyone bully, intimidate, shame, or guilt you into dimming your light or silencing your voice. **It's okay to live out loud!!!** You never know who you'll impact. We are so much more alike than we'd like to think. *(If only we knew just how much, there'd be less judgment and more understanding).* What if that one thing you were able to overcome despite the struggle, helps someone else. Despite your past, despite divorce, despite going through trials and tribulations, despite financial loss and humiliation, despite death in the family, despite illness, despite ALL the challenges... you can still SHINE!!!

I take you on this mental toughness journey so we can learn and grow together, support one another, and despite it all, still LIVE, LOVE, and LAUGH. Be you, BOLDLY! You're not for everyone—and that's okay—but be committed to showing YOUR tribe that they're not alone. Someone has been there, got through it, and is still standing. So, again, do not let anyone bully, intimidate, shame, or guilt you into dimming your light or silencing your voice. You're inspiring someone to push through what they once thought was impossible. You're doing this because you LIVE OUT LOUD!

— Monique Carter

Say Aloud: **I Will BOLDLY Shine. I Live OUT LOUD!!**

November

"I Will Be A Better Sister!"

The word sister has several meanings. A sister is a female—woman or girl—who shares the same parents as another. A sister is a female—friend or associate—sharing with you in the union of an organization or in a religious institution. It is important here to note that being a better sister goes beyond a woman's role or the responsibility often warranted through family relations. the act of being a sister also represents a partnership between women who are associated by sharing their innermost vulnerabilities.

Being a *better* sister calls for us women to connect and uplift one another through pain, purpose, and prayer. Being a better sister enables growth, cultivation, and it activates the power that is often lying dormant in the heart of a woman.

I will be a better sister by sharing truth, grace, discipline, and covering my sisters. Through sharing knowledge, correction, and faith, I will be a better sister because—SHE, ME, HER, I, US—WE are all connected!

> *If you have a sister, and she dies, do you stop saying you have one? Or are you always a sister, even when the other half of the equation is gone?"*
>
> Jodi Picoult

— Regina N Roberts

This Woman's Work (Today)

* List 10 women who have felt like sisters at some point in your journey.
* Compose a message to send to each of these women letting them know how much you appreciate them.
* Send these as your first step to being a better sister!

Love!

& Intimacy

December 1

I Will Love!!!

I will love because I know love. I will love because I feel love. I will transfer and accept love. Love is reciprocal. Love is shared among people, in communities, and within professions.

I will love because love is the pinnacle of living. Love is the cornerstone of life, relationships, and *self*-love. with all that love is, I will love myself and others. I will love even when it hurts because love builds strength. Love is who you and I were created to be.

— Regina N Roberts

December 2

I Will Put Love into What I Do

I will put love into what I do.
I will lead with love in mind.
I will put love into what I do so that others after me will gracefully and boldly wear the crown of LOVE.
I will put LOVE into what I do by expressing my vulnerabilities.
I will put love into what I do so that all things are done in excellence.
I will put love into what I do by stretching myself in areas of life that are uncomfortable but necessary for my growth.

★ When was the last time you examined your love in action?

— Regina N Roberts

December 3

" I Will Love Others Better "

When we think deeply about love and what it means, there are two examples that exceed our comprehension.

1. The love God has for us and
2. The picture of love found in 1 Corinthians 13.

Love is what we do, not what we say. Loving others better means we must be intentional to seek the greater good. This means learning and caring for the need of others without holding their sins, faults, issues, and failures as evidence to fight against them. in love, we don't keep record of wrong for judgment or argument's sake, but we extend grace, the same grace that we have received.

This Corinthian account of love, and the single greatest portrait of love in action explained in the gospels, shows us Christ, who gave what was needed instead of what was conveniently comfortable. Love is a sacrificial, vulnerable, unconditional verb expressed as a noun. It is an action expressed as something tangible. I must seek to know others in order to love them better. Rarely is love always pretty, always pleasant, and always desirable. However, love is always required.

Loving others better dictates that I take the time to discover others.

Love better. I must.
Love better. I will.

— Dr. Latisha D. Reeves Henry

Say Aloud: **I Will Love Others Better!!**

December 4

I Will Be Thoughtful

People are going through things every day that they may not talk about or care to express. People can be unknowingly careless and insensitive about the thoughts and concerns of others. Comforting words aren't always sincere, but developing a heart of thoughtfulness activates the meaning behind those words. No one cares how much you know until they know how much you care, so take time to be sure that those around you know how much you care.

True thoughtfulness is rare and beautiful. So…

Be thoughtful.

— Erika Harp

December 5

Loving Others is Easy, and I Vow to Do It Well

Loving others is easy. You flawlessly love the people you encounter. You are that strong friend who is always there for those you love or like, in one way or another, yet who is checking on you?

When you look over your life and see the people you impacted in one way or another, make those interactions count—not just to make yourself feel good, but be grateful for what God gave you the ability to do. You have a gift of love that is immeasurable. You were created in His image, and His image is LOVE.

There is One who is not only checking on you; He's carrying you when you can't move. His love for you is infinite and perfect. Sometimes, it doesn't feel that way, however, remember He's there consistently. His love doesn't fade, so love yourself first, and fill your cup with His greatness 'til it overflows like the living water given to the woman at the well.

God has given you purpose, drive, intent, and, most importantly, the ability to LOVE, so do it well!

— Stephanie Hamilton Muwunganirwa

December 6

I Will Open My Heart

I will open my heart to the possibilities of love,
new life lessons, and my destiny's legacy.
I will open my heart to new experiences,
new levels of love, and renewed love.
I will open my heart to a life that is lived without regret,
where I am free to think, free to serve, and free to create.
I will open my heart to accept all experiences—
I will view them as lessons learned.
I will open my heart to heal from brokenness and
disappointment.
I will open my heart to healthy expressions and progressive
experiences.
I will open my heart to the unknown and trust myself for
many unknowns to come.

The Lord will redeem those who serve him.
No one who takes refuge in Him will be
condemned.

Psalm 34:22

— Regina N Roberts

I Believe in Love *(Again)*

Sometimes I feel like I am the queen of heartbreak, and I don't just mean intimate relationships... My mother abandoned me shortly after birth, so I never felt loved by her. I bounced around from home to home from a very young age. That just made me feel unwanted. My dad was abusive, so he was just another parent who I felt didn't love me. I never made lasting friendships and the people that said they would stay always found some reason to leave. Love was a very unfamiliar word for me. Then, there came a period when it was time for me to be loved truly, and I just couldn't accept it.

When I got into this relationship, I heard of all the great things that His love was and all the things it could be. He told me that He would love me forever and unconditionally as a matter of fact. He told me He loved me despite all the mistakes I made. All the imperfect things that I saw in myself, He loved those things as well. All I could wonder was, *how*?

No one could love someone this broken—that's why everyone else had left. I found it hard to accept love from the people that He placed around me. They were supposedly going to love me differently than the love I had experienced before because they were imitating His love. After brushing off His love—and the love of His people—God finally told me, "Let your guard down. I have shown you my love, and that will never end." I finally found myself in a space where I could believe in love again. I no longer had to fear being loved because I was now in relationship with love Himself.

— Kenajawa LaShawn

December

There Is Someone Out There for Me

The story of Ruth and Naomi is a tragedy turned beautiful. Woman meets man, marries, and tragedy strikes, leaving her wounded and widowed. That happened to three women in the same family in a culture where women were not valued, and men were the breadwinners. Grieved and lonely, away from their homeland, one woman returns to her native land with the other woman, Ruth, choosing to stay with her mother-in-law Naomi. Together, they returned to Naomi's homeland.

Even in the most despairing situation, they chose to cling to the hope of family and community where God provided. That is where Ruth was found working.

The Moabite young woman who was loyal to Naomi was found gleaning in the field, working for food. She worked hard daily, and the beauty of her kind humility caught the eye of her Boaz. Love found her in the harshest of circumstances, faithful in service to Naomi with her heart available to God.

Sister-friend, don't give up on the possibility of a love that's just for you right here on earth. Obscurity is a great place to be found working faithfully, purpose-focused. Love can come when least expected. Boaz and Ruth were destined to meet before they knew of one another. Love found them both and connected them at the right time. the providence of God's hand brought them together.

There is someone out there looking, preparing just for you, and not even the craziness of life can stop what God has ordained.

— Dr. Latisha D. Reeves Henry

December 9

I Will Wait in Perfect Peace

Waiting is one of the hardest things that God ask us to do. However, when He requires us to wait, God is really asking us to serve. Isaiah 40:31 is a popular scripture that people go to when a friendly reminder is needed of God's promise to us. This scripture reminds us rely on His strength and not our own. I always thought that the word *wait* in this scripture meant to physically and mentally wait. However, to wait really means to serve.

When God speaks His promise to us, we should immediately ask Him how He wants us to serve His people. Through serving, you will find you gain renewed strength. by giving to others, your spirit will soar like an eagle because you will likely receive more out of serving then the recipient does in receiving and you will run— not walk—to additional opportunities to minister to others. While serving, you will find yourself too busy experiencing the glory of doing God's work that you will not realize the time it took for your own blessing to be realized. Learn to wait in the perfect peace of service to God's people.

— Cortney D. Surrency, AC-CHC

December 10

Pain Happens and Pain is Okay

*Find a place inside where there's joy,
and the joy will burn out the pain.*
                                        Joseph Campbell

*Pain happens to us all
Pain can happen silently
Pain happens to the proud
Pain happens to the humble
Pain happens to the rich
Pain happens to the poor
Pain happens to the drop out
Pain happens to the well-educated*

*He heals the broken hearted and
bandages their wounds*
                                        Psalms 147:3

Pain is Okay

— Kelly Gardner

Affirmation Journal
  ★ *What are the painful love areas in my life?*
  ★ *How am I assured that those things are okay?*
  ★ *How can I live in this comfort and keep being 'okay'?*

Say Aloud: **Pain Happens and Pain is Okay!**

I Will Never Let A Man Degrade ME

I pray that as you read this, you find the strength to assert your value on a man instead of allowing him to define it after the relationship begins.

I gave up self-respect and dignity to have you
Made myself a hypocrite for a fleeting desire
Destroyed myself, to build up your manhood
It all boils down to God not being enough
But no more, I promise to God
Please help me expose the evil inclinations of my heart
Would it be too much to ask for a fresh start?
Here, I lay it all
Repentance from a broken heart
Here I give you the broken pieces
With which I know you can make art
God, I underestimated you
With a heart full of doubt
But out of hard lessons
Come the best parts
—From Broken Pieces by Kenajawa Lashawn

This piece was written from a place of hurt, but I was looking for healing. I found myself allowing a man to define the value of my worth. I gave up pieces of me that I was not comfortable giving only with the hope of keeping him around.

— Kenajawa LaShawn

Say Aloud: **I Will Never Let A Man Degrade ME!**

December 12

"I Don't Need A Man to Define Me"

Society says you should be married by age 25 and planning for a family shortly after that, but that's not always reality. You see, women are raised and groomed to be wives and mothers, usually with little room for error. But what about the woman who doesn't want kids? Or what about the woman who doesn't want her life to be centered around her man? She is still strong. She is still capable, and her life is not over.

So, if you are that woman, at the next holiday dinner, tell your family to leave you alone about when you will get a man or have his children. Tell them the definition of a woman is not wrapped in a man, but being a woman means being your own person who happens to stand with a man if you choose. If you never get married, you are still a beautiful, successful, courageous, and strong woman who is more than able to do life on her own. You see, identity is not who you stand with, but identity is who you are!

Rise queen and rule your queendom!

— Chantell Williams

Affirmation Journal
* How does it feel to be an independent woman?
* How do I address the feelings of independence?
* How does my independence challenge me?
* How does my independence affirm me?
* How do I encourage other women to wear their independence well?

Chivalry is ALIVE!

Chivalry, alive? It would be naive to say totally, *yes*, but... "Yes, chivalry is alive and well." Saying *no* would mean we have failed as parents and society in assuming ALL young men are chivalrous. I believe *that* to be false—all men are not chivalrous. Every day, women—first and foremost, the MAMA's *(our first teachers)*—have an opportunity and responsibility to prepare their sons *(or male friends)* to show respect to them, to other girls and to women—young and elders alike. in respecting, teaching, and raising a male child, parents can example to their sons love, anger management, responsibility, and conversation *(how to talk to girls or women)*.

Raising a child is not a simple task. We all need help from time to time. As a navy wife, raising children on my own during certain timespans, meant I could not waiver—especially in their teen years! I also had other friends whose spouses were in port while mine was out, and it made for good balance in my household. Think... who do you have in your life to help you teach or show chivalry to your child? At what age does chivalry begin? What does chivalry mean to you? How does it look?

God trusts us to do our best, so what questions do you have of Him that will help you with this goal?

Ask, Seek, and Knock, for the answers will be given to you.

Oh, the love of a son!

— MommyV

December 14

Don't Be Afraid to Love

Don't be afraid to love again. I know there are many ways in which your perception of love has been tarnished, but don't allow your past to ruin what could happen in the future.

Take some time to heal yourself. Learn all that you need to learn from the last time love hurt you. Give God a try. He can show you that it's all worth it. And I am not just talking here; I am speaking from experience!
Love yourself enough to love again.

The most important thing I have gained is taking the time to learn myself. I learned to know the things that I love, so that next time, I will already be full of love and not seeking someone to fill me with love. Learning and loving myself also helps me to love the next person as well. I am not afraid to love again. I am not afraid to be loved again. If you are having a hard time feeling that you can love again, take your time. Heal from your past wounds and take some time before you approach love again. Just don't be afraid to love.

— Kenajawa LaShawn

Affirmation Journal

* How do I make and take the BEST love opportunities?
* How do I demonstrate my willingness to share in love?
* How do I show that I am not afraid to be loved?

December

"

Don't Be Afraid to Be Loved

"

The New King James translation of I John 4:18 says, "There is no fear in love; but perfect love casts out fear because fear involves torment. But he who fears has not been made perfect in love." Love is as beautifully complicated as people, each showing up with their own catalog of issues and baggage. This includes you and me.

Unfortunately, our attempts at love have left many of us battered, bruised, and emotionally abandoned. Some of us are afraid that if someone sees our reality, they will not stay. We find ourselves at opposite extremes controlled, stifled by our fear of being deeply wounded *(again)*. Sometimes, our love is desperately seeking, craving acceptance, and we give ourselves haphazardly, without thought, to situations where there can be no fruitfulness. Both extremes sabotage the chance for organic relationships to grow.

Let *this* sink in:

Don't be afraid to be loved.

Love is necessary. It is best expressed through freedom. People will do things that are hurtful, as do we, so pain cannot always be avoided. the character and intent behind actions must be scrutinized. Free yourself up through trusting that the Creator of love works all things together for your good. You don't have to put up walls or pretend that nothing affects you; just be.

When the Bible speaks of perfect love, it speaks of love that is complete—pure in its essence. That kind of love need not be feared. Instead, it should be embraced. This starts with being in tune with the Lover of our Souls. Our own love is based on a healthy understanding of the love of God. When we cultivate those relationships—with God and with ourselves—we show our readiness to receive love from others who are deserving of us. We are then free to give love in a healthy, mutual exchange.

We cannot allow fear to rob us. Walk in freedom and love like you mean it. Trust God to work out all the rest.

— Dr. Latisha D. Reeves Henry

December 16

" I Will Respect My Partner "

Respecting your partner embodies acts of kindness to welcome and understand the value of who they are.

I will respect my partner in a way that expresses the admiration I have for myself.

I will respect my partner in a way that uplifts, edifies, chastises, and protects them.

I will share in the appreciation of my partner's successes and failures, which have netted them the evolution of change.

I will respect my partner's hustle, grind, shine.

I will respect my partner's quest for self-love and discovery.

I will respect those aspects of my partner that I may not agree with because I find value in their thoughts, ideas, and creativity.

I will respect my partner and our boundaries.

I will respect my partner and provide space for my partner to flourish uniquely and differently from me.

I will respect my partner!!!!

— Regina N Roberts

Affirmation Journal

★ In what areas am I lacking respect from my partner?
★ In what areas am I lacking respect for my partner?
★ In what ways can I show my partner more respect?
★ How can I implement necessary changes?

December 17

I Will Practice Safe Sex

Practicing safe sex is beneficial for your sexual health. That is a given. You may not be aware, however, that the practice of safe sex is also beneficial for your mental health. Having the knowledge that you are free from STDs and STIs will place your mind at ease.

Using condoms is the most effective way to prevent sexually transmitted diseases and infections. If you have multiple partners, it may be helpful to get tested or visit your doctor between partners. Not only will this protect you, but it protects your partners as well.

Practicing safe sex can also mean protecting against pregnancy if you and your partner are not looking to have a child. There are many different forms of birth control available to women. If one form of birth control does not work for you, try a different form. the methods of birth control and types of contraception are so unique that there is something for everyone. to find what works best for you, talk to your doctor. You can even talk to your family or friends to see what worked for them. While talking about sex can often be uncomfortable, it is nothing to be ashamed of.

Be safe out there and get as much help as you need!

—— Arielle Griffin

Say Aloud: I Will Practice Safe Sex!

Lust Is Not the Same as Love

Movies, magazines, the internet, and television are all riddled with portraits of relationships and marriage. If we are honest, these things, coupled with childhood fairytales, helped to influence our grand expectations of love. Often, much of the imagery does not even depict true love. Love is rooted—it's grounded, unconditional, and grows deeper with time. Showing love means seeking the good of others.

Lust, on the other hand, is fueled by seeking the good of itself. It is consuming and devouring. Love is born of God. It suffers long, but lust is born of desires of the flesh. Acting in lust reduces people while love expands them. Lust also reduces what is sacred in love to mere envious yearning, and that can change on a whim.

Love and lust are both powerful forces, but lust does not endure. Learning the difference between the two is key to our emotional and spiritual health so that we don't pacify or satisfy temporary hunger, consumed and abandoned.

Acceptance, support, growth, protection, safety, sacrifice, and provision are part of the language of love, and that is commitment in action. Those are what we look for because even with the failures, issues, faults, and shortcomings of humanity, these traits and characteristics still reflect the essence of the picture we see of Christ. That is how we tell the difference. Does this stir my spirit, edify my being, or just whet my appetites? Lust is fleeting. Love is lasting. Lust is not the same.

— Dr. Latisha D. Reeves Henry

I Will Love Myself First Before I Expect My Mate to

Why should you require love from someone if you don't love yourself? How can someone know how to love you if you don't love you? Before you date, and especially before you marry, make sure you have the tools to give your mate so they can love you correctly. That starts with you doing the work to love yourself. Don't expect someone to give you something you don't know how to give yourself.

Too often, we expect someone else to jump through hoops for us. We want others to make heaven and earth move for us, not realizing we must be the first example of what we want others to be to us.

Musiq Soulchild sings, "Teach me how to love. Show me the way to get to your heart." *What's the path to your heart?* Don't hand someone a blank canvas and expect them to create a masterpiece without giving them the tools they need to do it.

— Coach Latoya Kight

Affirmation Journal

- ★ What does it mean for me to love myself?
- ★ How do I demonstrate love for myself daily?
- ★ How can I use my own love as a model of how I expect my mate to treat me?
- ★ What steps will I take to communicate my love for myself to my mate?
- ★ What steps will I take to communicate my love expectations?

Lovers May Leave, But True Love Is Everlasting

If someone told me that there is someone in this world who will love me forever—and unconditionally—I would not believe them. Then I realize that someone *has* shown me what an everlasting love looks like.

I consider what the cross means to me...

As He hung upon the cross, there was a name that crossed His mind. My name formed on His tongue as He gasped for His next breath. He said, "My child, I promise you strength, love, and courage. Today, your mother will forsake you, but tomorrow, you will gain many that will love you like their own. Today, your father will abuse you, but tomorrow your husband will love you with a love that I have trained him in. Many will abandon you, but I will forever be with you. My child, you're going to be stubborn in this thing called life. When you are ready for your tomorrow, I will be here with open arms. Today, I give my life," He said, "So that tomorrow, you may live."

Love is not dead.

Lovers may leave, but true love is everlasting.

— Kenajawa LaShawn

Say Aloud: **True Love Is Everlasting!**

December

"

I Won't Let Anything or ANYONE Get Between Me and My Mate

"

The question sometimes asked today is, "Why get married?" Why not just live together? What's a piece of paper anyway? How did you know? How do you know this is everlasting? 'Til death do us part love? So many other questions *(out of curiosity)* may pop up depending on the person's perspective of marriage.

I met my husband at 15 years of age, and by 16, we were engaged. My mother—having married early and divorced early as well—probably chuckled under her breath when we approached her. Her three mandatory rules for me were to 1, finish high school, 2, get some sort of higher education; and 3, get a job. Also, my now spouse had to reach E/4—a pay grade in the US Navy—to be able to afford me! Yes, we did *all* that, and we were married when I was 18 years old.

Our relationship has always been special to us. We knew from our parents' history, and that of some friends, that we were set for a long journey. There has never been a time when we thought of separating because we didn't get along, nor did we have difficulties so traumatic to cause us to split, but... *Did we really know?* "No." *Were there obstacles?* "Yes!" *Were we ever on two (or three) different pages?* "Yes!" *Were we* different *from other couples?* "We think so!"

In the beginning, while we thought my mother was being mean *(imagine that?)* because we were in a long, long distant relationship, we look back and realize that the time was training ground for us. We didn't want to be like our parents, so we knew there would need to be an effort on our part. Our promise to each other was simple: to talk it out; respect who we fell in love with and listen; give credence to the others feeling;

respect alone space; while we might have a lot in common, we're still individual persons; agree to disagree; our house and life was just too important. We were a team that has been blessed beyond our own expectations.

Here are some questions to consider:

Have you ever let someone else's opinion of you, or your relationship, affect how you respond to your mate? (Married or not) How many folks are you committed to, other than your spouse? Why? Do you see yourself building for a lifetime?

Real-life is NOT fantasy; know the difference before you commit to life! Find a person to mediate when things need to be refocused.

While there is so much more I could add here, and as of this writing, in 7 days, my spouse and I—now 68 & 70 years of age—will be celebrating FIFTY (50) years of marriage!! Yay God, who ordained us to experience #BlackLove on a day to day basis! God is good. Our love is solid!

— MommyV

December

It Is Okay to Spend Time with the One I Love

I am single, but I am not alone. for a long time, I dreaded being single. It seemed that everywhere I turned, someone was in a relationship. It left me questioning God, "Well, what am I supposed to do?" But, after a few tests and trials, I realized that this time of being single is not about being alone at all.

At the moment, I am in a committed relationship with God.

Once I realized this, I saw my singleness from a whole new perspective. Now, I am never alone; I spend a lot of time with the one I love. the quality time is amazing. I learn so much about Him and myself. It's helped me learn how to love others, and it prepares me for the relationship I will one day have. This relationship has bettered me. It taught me how to become whole before I try and add someone else into my life. God has helped me fall in love with myself in ways that I never imagined. This is truly the best relationship that I have ever been in. It gives me hope for the future relationship I will someday have.

— Kenajawa LaShawn

December

My Love Experience
Is Not Limited to Intimate Interactions

My Love Experience
is Not Limited to Intimate Interactions

In past relationships, I have always believed this to be true. However, within my current relationship, this proves to be even truer.

My significant other and I love to have fun and to be in the company of one another. We spend most of our time continuing to discover new things about one another by engaging in conversation. We enjoy having intellectual conversations over dinner or while sitting on the couch with a glass of wine. We also enjoy playing arcade games, bowling, or playing laser tag. We toss footballs, have *(plastic)* sword fights 😊, and play thumb war.

Intimate interactions should not define a relationship. They should only enhance it. I can honestly say that our relationship is not driven solely by sexual attraction. of course, this is an important aspect of most relationships, but it should not be the most important. In my opinion, preparing a meal for another person could be considered an intimate interaction. We do this quite frequently, and I consider this a fantastic time for us to bond.

In your own life, try to find more ways to share intimacy than just through physical or sexual encounters. Find ways to enhance your bond and love connections by deepening what you share with your mate just by being in their company.

— Arielle Griffin

December 24

" I Will Spend Quality Time with My Loved Ones "

Loved ones are those people in your life whom you find to be valuable. They are the people with whom you enjoy making memories and those you accountable to your truths. for many, loved ones are the family you were born into. for others, they are the family you've created along the way.

Time spent with loved ones should be esteemed as valuable for all and held in high regard. Spending time with your loved ones creates a practice or a trend, and it builds a sense of community that affects one's development.

If you find that the quality time you spend with the ones you love most is limited, I challenge you to make small steps toward creating and nurturing a platform that welcomes the practice of healthy quality time.

Quality time with loved ones breeds healthy relationships, open and direct communication, and a sense of self-worth and value. Enjoy it and your loved ones while you have the time!

— Regina N Roberts

I Will Be Good to My Parents

A parent is someone who takes care of, looks after and brings up another person. As a child, I can remember my parents were not an official couple. by the time of my birth, my parents' relationship had ended, yet both my mother and father advocated for each other. My dad's not being in the household brought about many different emotions for me, which altered the waves of our father-daughter relationship. As life progressed, the integrity and character of my mother never wavered, nor did her demeanor compliment my own foolishness. Instead, my mother encouraged me to foster a relationship with my father by simply modeling her relationship with my father. So, despite my own yearnings, disappointment hand faults, my mother continued to encourage goodness toward my father. Moreover, because of my mothers' outward advocacy for my dad, this expressed what it meant for me to be good to my parents.

Life always has a way of teaching many lessons. I have learned to be good to my parents through their own devotion and partnership in co-parenting because of how each parent advocated for the other parent. Parents are often penalized for what they don't do, yet growing up with my parents taught me to appreciate that parents simply do their best without having a roadmap on how to parent.

Food for thought:

Celebrate your parents for their decision to birth you. Celebrate your parents for their efforts in doing their very best to the best of their knowledge. Parenting is one role that is often judged by those of us without any amount of training ourselves. Forgive your parents and be good to them. One day, you will parent a child, a tribe, or even a nation. Get the best learning that you *now* by learning to be good to your parents.

— Regina N Roberts

I Love My Mother.
I Love the One Who Gave Me LIFE.

She's my mother, the one who gave me life.
She carried me safely until her womb gave me sight.
The rhythm of her heart was like music to my ears.
The essence of her smell calmed all my fears.
She's my mother, the one who sacrificed her life for me.
She was my breathing breath, and through her, my eyes could see.
With her nurturing breast, she fed me, and I grew strong.
The sound of her voice soothed my soul like the melody of a song.
She's my mother, the Earth Angel-God gave her as my guide.
The wisdom that flows from her heart is where love abides.
Her arms securely embrace me with all the love I need,
And in her hands, a tender rod to keep me on my knees.
She's my mother. No one can take her place.
Images of her children are etched upon her face.
Her prayers reach heaven and the angels bid her cry,
For she is blessed, and her voice is known on high.
She's my mother. I will kiss her while the sun shines.
Tomorrow is not promised. Only God keeps her time.
Mother, while I have you close and your eyes look my way,
I shout from my heart,
I Love You Always!

–Minister Gail Engram

27 December

I Appreciate My Family

Family is everything. You most certainly can't survive in life without family. Sometimes, they're given to you by birth and sometimes by life. No matter how much you try to get away from them, no matter how much you try to ignore them, no matter how much you don't want to claim them *(lol)*. You are stuck with them!!! Life with it! Love it!

You don't get to choose your family. They are given to you. So now that you have them, turn your power to *appreciate* them, not because they've done anything for you. Appreciate your family just because you are blessed to have people in your space that will always be there for you.

Don't ever get to a point where you think you don't need family. Family is always needed. Thank God that He blessed you with family. They are there when you cry. They are there when you laugh and everything in between. There is nothing like family, so always remember to value them.

Family is everything!

— Coach Latoya Kight

This Woman's Work (Today)
 ★ List your top 3 favorite family members.
 ★ List the 3 family members who deserve more of your time.
 ★ Schedule time this week to call each of these people.

This Woman's Work (This Month)
 ★ Schedule out times for the next 3 months to contact these people bi-weekly.

I Am in Touch with My FEELINGS

Time has taught me not to ignore or suppress my feelings. Whether they be angry, sad, good or bad, those feelings matter. I can't just block them out. My personal growth and development depend on me properly dealing with and learning how to react to my feeling.

For quite from time, I would act as if I didn't feel. I thought I was protecting myself from being hurt. This charade didn't prevent me from being hurt. It simply caused me to bottle up all those negative feelings because I didn't know how to deal with them. That was completely unhealthy for me, so eventually, I had to dig deep and not only accept those negative feelings for what they were, but I had to also understand why. *Why do I feel this way? Why does this situation affect me so much? Why am I allowing this situation to affect me?* Once I could get a better understanding of my inner workings, I could also better react to those feelings.

As I grow as a woman, I learn to be more in touch with my feelings, and I'm a better person because of it.

— Brittany Whigham

This Woman's Work (Today)

★ List out 3 methods you use to express feelings.
★ List out 3 methods you could add to this list.

"

I Am Rich in Love

"

To be rich in love is to have an abundant or mass amount of value that you are willing to give *and* receive.

Richness in love is an expression that says you have acknowledged the love that resides within you as it is shared with others. to be rich in love means you have mastered an expression of healthy love, even to those with whom you have had negative experiences. This depth of love shows that you have forgiven those who formerly persecuted you. It shows that you have forgiven the faults of others that have unfairly targeted you. to be rich in love means to be aware of your capacity to love others—and yourself—without judgment. Richness in love provides a bounty that only love can give as well as an openness of connection that only love can receive.

— Regina N Roberts

Affirmation Journal

- ★ How do I show that I rich in love?
- ★ What are my love issues?
- ★ What are the most pressing issues that need resolving?
- ★ How will my resolution of these issues change my life?
- ★ How will resolving these issues increase my richness in love?

Say Aloud: **I Am Rich in Love!**

30
December

I Walk in Love

I walk in Love
I walk in Peace
I walk in Passion
I walk in God's Love
I walk in the love of my singleness
I walk in the love of my marriage
I walk in the love of my children
I walk in love with an open mind
I walk in love with an open heart
I walk in love with open arms

Love is patient and kind.
Love is not jealous or boastful or loud or
rude. It does not demand its own way. It is
not irritable, and it keeps no record of
being wronged. It does not rejoice about
injustice but rejoices about injustice but
rejoice whenever the truth wins out. Love
never gives up, never loses faith, is always
hopeful and endures though every
circumstance.

1 Corinthian 13:4-7

I walk in Love

— Kelly Gardner

Affirmation Journal
* *How do I show that I am willing to receive love?*
* *How do I show that I am willing to give love?*
* *How do healthy expressions of love help me through life?*

I Want to Love Like Jesus Loves

Jesus has the greatest love story of all time! Him dying for our sins was the most selfless act of love any human being could possibly do for another. If you believe that He was sent to earth to be a living example of God's love, then you must believe that you can love how Jesus loves! Being made in the image of God means we have the opportunity to do the things He did, including having the temperament He had. He dealt with mean and hurtful people, but He was able to consistently look past the person's earthly actions by focusing on the fact that the offender is God's child. **Whom God loves, we must also love.** We require grace daily. However, this isn't a concept we easily grasp when it's time to give grace back to others.

Look daily for opportunities to give grace. Next time you have a conflict with someone, do something nice for them. Let the Holy Spirit guide your actions, and what you will find is that they will receive your kindness in such a way that it will bless your life, too! You may not love like Jesus 100% of the time, but you will find that the more you provide grace, the more God receives the Glory!

Amen.

— Cortney D. Surrency, AC-CHC

but wait!
there's more

Additional reader-only content including worksheets, workbooks, writing prompts and journals can be found at http://ShShares.com. Visit us for resources on this book and others within the Change Your Posture series.

I would LOVE to personally connect with you!

Attn: Coach D Nicole!
Sh'Shares NETWORK
PO BOX 13202
Jacksonville, FL 32206

www.CoachDNicole.com
www.ShShares.com

It is my sincere prayer that you were blessed by the contents of this book. I look forward to securing our connection well into the future!

Thank you for your GREATNESS!

Coach D Nicole is a very charming and spirited first-class professional who is passionate about encouraging, supporting and coaching others within their personal lives and business endeavors. As a transformational life coach, she is most loved for her wit, boisterous personality, direct and upfront coaching style, and generous, authentic smile!